ONE WAY TO

WRITE ANYTHING

ONE
WAY
TO
WRITE
ANYTHING

Helena M. Barrett

BARNES & NOBLE BOOKS
A DIVISION OF HARPER & ROW, PUBLISHERS
New York, Cambridge, Philadelphia,
San Francisco, London, Mexico City, São Paulo, Sydney

FIRST EDITION

Designed by C. Linda Dingler

Library of Congress Cataloging in Publication Data

Barrett, Helena M.
  One way to write anything.
  Includes index.
  1. Abstracting. I. Title.
PE1477.B3 1982   808′.042   81-47817
ISBN 0-06-463551-1 AACR2

82 83 84 85 86 10 9 8 7 6 5 4 3 2 1

"A thought must tell at once, or not at all."

—WILLIAM HAZLETT

CONTENTS

INTRODUCTION
ONE WAY ...

About *One Way to Write Anything:*
   People write for three reasons:

1. They are required to fulfill an assignment for high school, college or business.
2. They feel the need to express an idea.
3. They want to make money.

   Very few people write only for their own enjoyment, for the pleasure of writing is minimized unless it can be shared with others.

   Whatever the reason for writing, however, ease of writing enhances the process. When you know what you are doing in determining the subject, gathering material, and structuring the paper, you develop the confidence that not only tones you for a fine job of writing but also imparts to the reader a certain respect for what you have to say. You may not change the reader's mind—if that is your intent—but you will make him think about your interpretation of the subject. He may not be able to journey to beautiful spots that you have visited, but he'll share the experiences through your picturing them. He might never have become aware of certain conditions or situations but for your informing him. The reader may be able to understand you better after reading something you have written.

One Way to Write Anything is a step-by-step guide designed to assist:

- the high school senior who needs a way to lessen the gap yawning between high school English and the demands of college writing
- the college student who feels weak in writing skills and needs confidence in undertaking written assignments
- the secretary who is called upon to write a report or a business letter
- the business person who must write a speech
- anyone who needs to compose an important business letter
- the angry citizen who wants to write a letter to the editor or forum in the newspaper
- the concerned person who has an idea he believes in and wants to clarify for others
- the lecturer, minister, or other public speaker
- the writer who needs a structure for the writing of articles intended for publication

The basic system of writing demonstrated is the accepted foundation for all writing. Once you have mastered this basic pattern, you'll be able to present your work in a style that is a reflection of your personality, an interpretation of your own thinking on a given subject. Therein lies reader interest. It is personal. Readers like to know what others have said, but they are more interested in what you, a contemporary, possibly a peer, have to say about a particular subject. They want your "side" of the issue, your explanation of the condition, your view of the situation.

The creativity you apply to what would otherwise be a ho-hum assignment, report, or speech is very important, but the authoritative impact will be strongest when you write with understanding of the subject and confidence of structure.

Follow the steps in *One Way to Write Anything* to gain the confidence and authority of writing that will cause your reader to complete the reading of your paper with a feeling of thorough satisfaction.

You will encounter other methods of doing some of the papers discussed. Teachers, professors, and superiors may all have their personal preferences as to technique and format. When you are studying under or working for other people, by all means follow the procedures they require. The purpose of *One Way to Write Anything* is to provide you with a foundation when you have no one else to give you guidance or when you need to supplement or reinforce the instructions you have been given.

PART ONE
...TO WRITE...

1

GATHERING MATERIAL

Writing is work. No question about it. For that very reason, it should be approached in a workmanlike manner. You must know what tools and techniques are available and you must become skilled in their use. You must be willing to observe people around you, the problems of the day, the needs of business, the moral structure of the times. You must learn to organize your information so that it is relevant to the specific subject you are exploring.

Now, this is not a description of the professional writer. Very few people are interested in making writing a career, although this book is a good place to begin if this is your goal. It is safe to say, however, that all of you at one time or another will have to write reports, business letters, research papers, book reviews, and term papers for high school, college, or continuing education classes, or to meet the requirements of your job.

Before you get the idea that writing is far too difficult for you, write a paper step by step as outlined in this book and discover for yourself how well within your ability good writing really is. Select your own subject and follow through each step of the process until you have completed the piece. By doing the work yourself, you will learn how to approach any writing project you may encounter.

Ready? Go!

SUBJECT

"What shall I write about?"

This is the wail of most beginning writers—and some professionals—who expect to find a treasure chest of ideas handed to them along with the assignment.

Sometimes you will be given a subject on which to write in order to fulfill a specific requirement of a client, professor, or employer. It might be a business report, a letter, or a proposed solution to a given problem. More often, you will be expected to choose your own subject, and the responsibility of choosing can sometimes be the most difficult step of all.

It needn't be, for you have three file drawers from which to choose an interesting subject: Memory, People, Library. Before searching for material you must select a subject from one of these drawers.

Maybe you had an interesting experience you'd like to share or lived in a beautiful house you want to describe. If so, you'll make your selection after looking through the Memory file. All your experiences are gathered there for you to select, organize, and present in support of the subject you have chosen. Opinions, interpretations, new ideas wait there for you.

Your interest may lean in the direction of the new car that does not use a combustible engine or to the question of individual rights and how far those rights extend before they encroach on the rights of others. You may decide to draw entirely from the People file for this type of subject and gather your material through interviews with local experts or friends who are to some extent involved in the subject field.

You may have wondered about the hubbub on solar energy, or wanted to know what a bathyscaph is, or Mercato's Project. You may have wondered who Josephus was, or Saki, or Nietzsche. You may want to better understand the Biblical promise to the Jews or the origins of the Arab people. If so, your Library file will be a storehouse of subject ideas that require further investigation. Once you've selected a topic from the Library file, you'll read what the authorities, ancient and contemporary, have to say on the subject, and your paper will be the result of your study.

Maybe you have a pet peeve that digs at you or an opinion that you would like to discuss. If so, you'll want to dip into all three files to explore your opinions, to prove your point, and to develop your findings into a valuable paper.

As you go through the selection process, keep in mind that you should be sufficiently interested in the subject so that the hours you spend gathering material and writing will be enjoyable.

LIMITING THE SUBJECT

Now that you have selected your subject, learn how to limit it so that the idea can be written about satisfactorily in the word limit you have allowed yourself: in this case 2,000 to 3,000 words, or 8 to 12 typed pages. Weigh the content. Is it too rich to be confined to that word limit? Is it too skimpy to allow you to write more than two paragraphs? Make sure you have sufficient material to examine the point you want to make and conclude it logically.

For instance, consider the subject of Aviation. Volumes have been written on this subject. How could you possibly expect to compress it into a 2,000-word paper? Begin by examining the various facets of aviation. You might focus on noise pollution caused by large planes, safety factors in depending on instruments for flight directions, physical requirements for pilots, time lag for passengers, dangers of sonic booms, air traffic congestion, comfort of new passenger planes, or the pros and cons of discount fares from the viewpoint of the airlines. The possibilities are limitless.

As stated above, this single topic must be rich with ideas but not so rich that it will require more space than you plan to give it. It must be to the point, but not so skimpy that you'll have told all in the first two paragraphs. To judge the worth of the focal idea, you must write a statement that promises what the paper is all about. This sentence has several names: statement of fact, statement of truth, thesis, and so on. For this book, it will be referred to as the Statement of Purpose.

STATEMENT OF PURPOSE

The Statement of Purpose is a simple sentence that concerns one point only. Its purpose is to keep you on track so you stick to the topic you promised to discuss and end on the same subject you started with. It is the hub of the entire paper.

Do you know what you want to say? Write it down. Now study the thought that inspired you to select this subject. Does the sentence you wrote say what you want it to? Remember, the Statement of Purpose is one of the writer's basic and absolutely necessary tools. Get it right *before* you do any of your research or try to write anything. After you've researched the subject, you may rewrite the statement to strengthen your point, but you must have a working Statement of Purpose to direct your research.

Why is this necessary? Have you ever looked up a word in the dictionary and in the process found another word that caught your attention? You stopped to read about the off-the-track word and later, if you remembered, went back to the word you had planned to find. The problem is more severe in research on a limited subject. You find during the process that other equally interesting facets appear; interesting terms poke up their heads. Fascinating human interest stories, intriguing experiments, and so on, send you scooting into other areas, probably related to your general subject but not supportive of the one idea you chose to discuss. If you don't establish your Statement of Purpose at the outset, you'll get lost, change direction, and end up wasting a lot of valuable time by having to go back to the beginning and start all over.

Write your Statement of Purpose. Look at it. Think it through. Insist that it say exactly what you started out to discuss.

If you find it extremely difficult to confine your purpose to one sentence, you probably don't really know what you want to say. It is easy to think about a subject in great detail and still not pin down the core of the idea. Be honest in your thinking. What is that one important point you want to make? What do you want to get across to your reader? What is your reason for writing the paper? If other ideas keep nagging at you and appear to be equally important in spite of their lack of support, jot them down briefly and file them for future papers you may want to write. Don't dally over them at this point; simply write them down and put them away so that you can keep your mind on your Statement of Purpose.

Suppose, for instance, that you are interested in writing on the subject of Penology. You've considered the many aspects of the subject, and you've decided to focus on Pre-parole. Your Statement of Purpose might read:

> Pre-parole deinstitutionalizes prisoners so that they are aware of changes on the "outside" before they reenter society.

This single point or idea promises your reader what he can expect in your paper.

Maybe your interest is in Business Employment, and you select the personnel problem of hiring employees. If so, your Statement of Purpose might read:

> The personnel managers of most corporations make a fetish of the college degree as a requirement for jobs.

One of the big problems in education is Johnny's inability to read, and you want to find out what is at back of this fact. In a sweeping statement the assertion includes: "too many students," "too few teachers," "poor reading materials," "lack of interest"—you name it and "it" falls into the Johnny-can't-read category. You can find arguments to support any one of the reasons, so it is up to you to determine which one you are going to discuss. Your Statement of Purpose might read:

> Johnny's inability to read too often stems from his own lack of responsibility.

CONTROLLING IDEA

In each Statement of Purpose you must have a Controlling Idea that pinpoints your reason for writing the paper. It is the focal point, the important idea you plan to prove or expose or discuss.

Look again at the Statements of Purpose we just discussed. Study them. Determine the focus, the Controlling Idea of the sentence. Underline that one idea within the sentence.

> Pre-parole deinstitutionalizes prisoners so that <u>they are aware of changes on the "outside" before they reenter society</u>.

The importance or focal point of this statement concerns familiarizing prisoners with new social customs, new advances in technology, new fashions, and so on, that have developed during their years of incarceration. You aren't discussing any other features of prison life or attitudes of either the prisoner or the citizen. Your only purpose is to let the reader know about this aspect of Pre-parole.

> The personnel managers of most corporations <u>make a fetish of the college degree as a requirement for jobs</u>.

Again, you aren't exploring the job of the personnel manager, the general requirements for jobs in corporations, or unemployment. You are zeroing in on the idea that personnel managers think that a college degree stands high above every other employment requirement.

> Johnny's inability to read too often stems from his own lack of responsibility.

The Controlling Idea makes it quite clear that your paper is going to ignore the many other reasons suggested for Johnny's inability to read and that you are going to discuss only Johnny's lack of responsibility as it affects his ability to read. You are not discussing his inability to read; rather you're focusing on one cause of his inability.

Now how about the Statement of Purpose you wrote? Make sure that the idea within the sentence, the Controlling Idea that you underlined, is truly the one point you plan to clarify and prove. Don't let a couple of unsuccessful tries discourage you. It's a difficult task, but you shouldn't settle for anything less than the correct focal point. You must know what you want to say.

Work with your statement until you have defined the purpose and focus of your writing. Never fall heir to the lazy attitude that allows you to write a paper of words just to complete an assignment. Say something or don't write.

INFORMATION

Your next responsibility is to find the information that will support the Controlling Idea of your Statement of Purpose. To do this, go into the file drawers mentioned earlier: Memory, People, Library. (Because of the details it involves, the Library is treated separately in Chapter 2.)

Memory

The first and most convenient drawer from which to find ideas is Memory. All your experiences, thoughts, loves, hates, interests, everything that happens to and about and with and for you, is tucked away in your memory to be selected and used in the manner that is best for you. Some things you tuck far back in the darker corners because you don't want to think about them again. Others, by varying degrees, come to light and are worthy of reliving in your thoughts, and these are the things you'll review. Your memories are a reflection of who you are. Select one that you think might interest another person and relive it on paper. Re-create it in full color and with a new surge of your own interest. Use it as a basis for a fictional report such as an anecdote to support a point in your paper, or use it as a case history that helps prove your statement.

"But nothing I've ever done is interesting," you say.

Maybe it is no longer interesting to you, for you are continually living new experiences that are fresher and more immediately interesting. The fact that you are tired of something, however, does not necessarily dull another's interest, unless *you* approach it with an attitude of apathy. Continuous curiosity creates interest in another's life. Your reader may have had a similar experience and want to compare stories. Maybe your reader hasn't been exposed to the kinds of adventures or interests you have had. Through your writing, you can share some of your own experiences with him.

Certainly, after sifting through the jumble of your memory— you probably haven't put it in order for years—you can't say that you lack material. On the contrary, you will have to be most selective. If the subject choice is yours, select an experience that you really enjoyed or that left a mark on you.

Remember the time you were standing on State and Randolph in Chicago and the change of lights caught a crippled girl in the middle of State Street? How about the time you were asked to play golf with Arnold Palmer because you happened to be there? How did you feel when you sold your first article? You have a thousand more interesting ideas than these. Not very exciting? The more you think about your memories, the more interesting they become.

Relax! Good ideas come faster if you don't probe and push yourself. Don't even bother to evaluate them; all that will come later.

The Memory file is very important, for it is here that you will find the initial ideas that will help you determine a subject or help you flesh out your structure. However, you must add to it in order to draw upon it later.

Recording Ideas

It is important that any thought that crosses your mind concerning your selected topic, no matter how fleeting, be written down so that you can work with it in the writing process. You must record what you do know about the topic.

Let's start the work properly, the way you will work with each file.

Purchase a supply of 3 × 5 cards. If you prefer, you can cut your own "cards" from ordinary typing paper. Fold an 8½ × 11-inch sheet of typing paper bottom to top and side to side. Cut on the creases. This gives you four pieces of paper, each approximately the size of a 3 × 5 card. These "cards" aren't as substantial to work with as the standard kind, but often they are more readily handy when you want to record your latest thought.

Write with a pen. When you shuffle the cards, as you are bound to do in the process of organizing and outlining, penciled notes will smudge and become very difficult to read. Ideas have a way of being elusive, and once you have written one down, the very act satisfies the mind. It is possible that your note is the only thing that will help you recall the thought. Smudged, the note means nothing and the thought is lost.

For every thought that comes to you, therefore, write a note, in ink, on a card as shown in Figure 1.

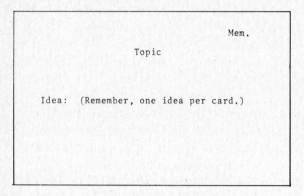

Figure 1.   Notecard: memory

The "Mem." in the upper right-hand corner of the card indicates that the idea comes from the Memory file. At the top-center of the card, place the topic. This is a classification of related thoughts. For instance: You are writing about the experiences of a family move from Denver to Los Angeles. On the cards, you'll write down everything that happened, not in sequence but in the order you remember specific incidents. Identify the note by writing the topic: injury on van, dinner first night out, Grand Canyon, cleaning carpets of house you moved from, packing antiques, notifying the utility company, and so on. If several happenings belong under the same topic, be sure to record each one on a separate card. When you classify each idea as you go along, you'll find that organizing the information later on will be no problem.

Begin with about twenty-five cards. On the first card write the word SUBJECT and identify it. If you have a tentative title, write it on a second card. Label the third card STATEMENT OF PURPOSE and write your statement. Underline the Controlling Idea, that one point you are promising your reader you will explain. You must have no fewer than ten cards with notes but should have twenty or more. Remember that it is always easier to write when you have so much material that you must be selective about what you include. When you accumulate only a skimpy amount of information, you are hard put to find enough information to write anything and are likely to resort to padding. "Padding" is stuffing your writing with inconsequentials, things that prove nothing and generally say nothing. Such writing will take all the interest out of the work for you and will turn the reader off instantly.

When you have written on your cards every idea pertaining to your subject, you're ready to begin organizing. We'll talk about how you can combine this material into a fine paper after we have taken a look at the other two files (see Chapter 3).

People

The People file offers some of the most interesting material you will find for your paper. It may be a member of your family, a priest, a police officer, a jeweler, a paperhanger, a teacher. People love to talk about themselves or about the subject they know best. Talk to a coach about his football team's chances in their league, or about his prophecies of the NFL winner. Talk to an architect about the new all-wood house. Talk to a showman about the trends in new theatrical productions, a race driver about the best training for an average driver, a professional gambler about the gaming business. Talk to any expert in your subject field and you are bound to get some gems for your paper.

Interviewing

Gathering information for the People file, however, requires that you interview people, that is talk to people with a definite point in mind. Before you set out for an interview, make some preparations. You must respect your interviewee's knowledge and time.

Research your subject so that you can talk about it with a modicum of ease and can ask intelligent questions along the way. It is wise to write down some of the questions in a small notebook so that you won't have to try to remember them under the pressure of recording what's being said. It is also important to learn something about the person you are going to interview. Is he an expert on the subject? Is he now active in the subject field? What is his professional status? Let him know that you are interested in him as well as in the information he can give you.

Assess the amount of time you will need for the interview. When you call for an appointment, ask him if he can give you that much time. Make sure that you do call for an appointment. Don't just drop in on a busy person.

Let the interviewee do the talking. You can prod him now and again by asking a question or mentioning something you have read or heard about the subject. He is the expert, so ask his opinion. Listen very carefully to what he says.

Professional writers learn to take a minimum of notes while actually interviewing for fear the person will "freeze" and won't be able, or willing, to tell very much about himself or the subject of the interview. You are not a professional writer, however, so you must fall back on note-taking. Train yourself to remember speech patterns, mannerisms, definite attitudes, but take lots and lots of notes. They will give you the authenticity you need when you begin writing.

Can you use a tape machine during an interview? It is possible if the interviewee doesn't object. Get his permission before turning it on; otherwise, if he dislikes the idea of having his voice recorded, he may refuse to allow the interview. Don't try to be clever and use a tape recorder you can hide. A person must be aware that he is being recorded.

The most important thing about using information from an interview is accuracy. If the interviewee qualifies a statement, record it as a qualification. "I think," "Perhaps," and the like are qualifications, not facts. Respect both his words and the meaning he intends to convey.

Upon concluding the interview, you must prepare the material for use. You probably have worked out a kind of shorthand to aid you in writing your notes. Generally, when these notes get "cold"—when you let them stand overnight or when several days pass before you can get back to them—much is lost. While the interview is still fresh in your mind, go someplace where you can work.

First, make a Bibliography card which records the source of the information, as shown in Figure 2.

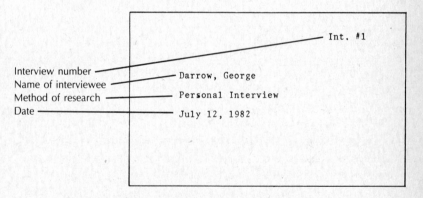

Figure 2.   Bibliography card: interview

Then transcribe all your notes, putting one idea on one notecard as indicated in Figure 3. Remember to record the interview number in the upper right-hand corner along with the appropriate topic heading. (The second interview, of course, has similar notecards, labeled "Int. #2," corresponding to the second Bibliography card.) Use notecards to record any interesting mannerism, distinctive attitude, or different approach to the subject, but be sure to identify them for what they are: mannerisms, and so on.

NOTE: When you are quoting your interviewee verbatim, place his words in quotation marks so that there is no confusion as to who said what when the time comes for you to write.

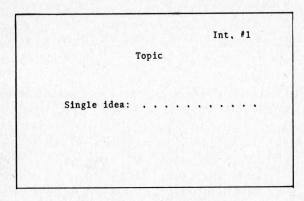

Figure 3.   Notecard: interview

When writing your text, be sure to identify the interviewee by name unless he prefers to be anonymous. Readers dislike the writer's using a vague "It was alleged . . ." or "A fireman expressed . . ." This falls into the impersonal "they" classification, that faceless "group" that knows all, says all, and carries little authenticity.

Again, we'll go into the method of combining all of the information and weaving it into the writing of your paper in Chapter 3. But first, let's look into the third drawer: the Library file.

2

THE LIBRARY

The third file is the Library. Here you will store your notes on all the facts and authorities that will help you prove your Statement of Purpose. You'll find material both against and in support of your Controlling Idea, and that is as it should be. It is important that you know something of the "other" side so that you can weigh your findings and judge the validity of your Purpose.

In the preliminary steps outlined in Chapter 1, you chose a subject, focused on a central topic, wrote your Statement of Purpose, and underlined the Controlling Idea. You learned to equip yourself with notecards and pen. You now need one more thing, an expansion envelope complete with a tie to fasten it. Keep your cards in this envelope, for to lose a single card may throw you back hours in your preparation for writing.

You are now ready to go to the library, where chances are you will become a fixture until you hand in your paper.

LOCATING SOURCE MATERIAL

Most of you have used the library and know how to find the information you need, but let's review the call numbers for books. Two systems are employed by the libraries to classify books: the Library of Congress Classification and the Dewey Decimal System.

Library of Congress Classification

A	General Works	M	Music
B	Philosophy and Religion	N	Fine Arts
C	History and Auxiliary Sciences	P	Language and Literature
D	Foreign History and Topography	Q	Science
		R	Medicine
E–F	American History	S	Agriculture
G	Geography and Anthropology	T	Technology
		U	Military Science
H	Social Science	V	Naval Science
J	Political Science	Z	Bibliography and Library Science
K	Law		
L	Education		

Dewey Decimal System

000	General Works	500	Pure Science
100	Philosophy	600	Applied Science
200	Religion	700	Art and Recreation
300	Social Science	800	Literature
400	Linguistics	900	History

NOTE: Specific divisions are indicated by further numbers which you will find at the upper left-hand corner of the card in the card catalogue.

You should also become acquainted with the *Reader's Guide to Periodical Literature,* the *International Index, Poole's Index to Periodical Literature,* and special indexes concerned with specific subjects.

Source material may be searched for in three ways in the card catalogue:

1. Title card
2. Subject card
3. Author card

The call numbers in the upper left-hand corner will be the same in all three cases.

BIBLIOGRAPHY CARDS

You must make a check of available material before you begin taking notes. To do this, make a card for each book you find that carries information on your specific subject (see Figure 4). If your Bibliography list shows you that sufficient information is available either in the library or through its lending facilities, you may begin your research. If the information is scant, select another subject. Further research may take more time than you can easily afford, and time is usually a crucial factor.

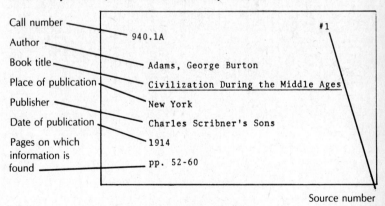

Call number — 940.1A #1
Author —
Book title — Adams, George Burton
Place of publication — Civilization During the Middle Ages
Publisher — New York
Date of publication — Charles Scribner's Sons
Pages on which information is found — 1914
pp. 52-60
Source number

Figure 4.   Bibliography card: library

The Bibliography card—the listing you make for each book, or other source, you use—has further use. It provides the information you will need for footnotes or other methods of documentation and for the Bibliography section that appears at the end of the paper.

It is important to include all this information on a card for each book you use. If for any reason you need to go back to the source, you'll know from the Bibliography card which book it is from, where to find it, and the exact pages on which you first found the information. This will save you from considerable frantic searching.

NOTE: In Figure 4, the number in the upper right-hand corner indicates that this is the first book, the first source from which you took material. Circle the number. This number indicates each source as you use it: #1, #2, #3, and so on. The corresponding number is placed on each notecard bearing information from the specific source.

NOTECARDS

Making notecards is an important step in your preparation for writing any paper based on researched material. On these cards you write all the information you select to reinforce your Controlling Idea (see Figure 5).

In the upper right-hand corner of each notecard, place the number that corresponds to the number recorded in the upper right-hand corner of the Bibliography card for its source. Each idea or piece of information from the source will bear the same number on the notecard. You can thus go to the source at any time you have some question about the information. This is insurance, though you may not need it often.

More important, when the time comes for writing the paper and documenting the material, all the information you'll need

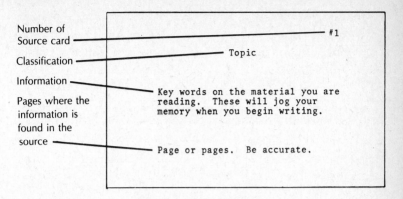

Number of Source card ——————————— #1

Classification ——————— Topic

Information ———

Pages where the information is found in the source ———

Key words on the material you are reading. These will jog your memory when you begin writing.

Page or pages. Be accurate.

Figure 5. Notecard: Library

is on the Bibliography card indicated by the notecard. The source and the information are tied together.

Note-taking

It is so easy to copy material directly from a source, promising yourself that you will rephrase it into your own words when the time comes to write the paper. Or you may decide that the author wrote the material in the only way it could have been written. And who are you to think you can improve it! Don't fool yourself.

In the first place, by the time you are ready to write the paper, you will have forgotten whether or not you copied the note or put the material into your own words. And having already invested so much time and effort, you probably won't bother to go back and check. This is your first mistake, and it can be avoided quite easily if you take the time to record the information on your notecard in the proper manner.

Secondly, the source author expressed his own feelings, his own ideas, his own viewpoint in his writing and must be given full credit. With a little extra thought and effort on your part, you'll discover that you can write the paper interestingly in your own words and still give the source author his due credit.

Be honest in writing your notecards. If you take an excerpt from the work, document it; if you lift an idea developed by the source author, document it. For the rest of the material, read it, assimilate it, and put down only the key words that will help you recall the information when necessary. Having only key words, you will be called upon to flesh out the ideas in your own words.

Doing this does not, however, relieve you of the responsibility of giving the author credit for any thought that is uniquely his. And make sure that you retain the author's opinion. Lifting a thought from the author's text and weaving it into your own paper may very well change the author's intent. It is up to you to make sure that you never change the author's viewpoint.

Why all this fuss about the author's work? Plagiarism! Ever hear of the word? "Plagiarism" is the stealing of another's ideas and passing them off as your own. The law concerning plagiarism must be understood by all writers. The same principles cover books, articles, short stories, music, lyrics, inventions, philosophical ideas, and so on.

In high school, plagiarism is usually punished by severe reprimand and the loss of the grade. Colleges usually aren't as easy. They look upon plagiarism as outright theft and assume rightly that a college student knows what he has done. For such an unnecessary act, the college student not only loses his grade but often is expelled from the college.

Professionally, plagiarism is taboo! Period. A plagiarist can be taken to court and heavily fined. His reputation suffers or is destroyed. Plagiarism is seldom committed accidently; it is a deliberate act.

Public domain helps out the researcher. Material that is common knowledge or that has outlived its copyright is considered available for the use of the public and is known as PD, or public domain. It is not plagiarism to use this material because it does not belong to one person or party. However, it should be documented; you must not present another person's material as your own.

Often you will paraphrase from the source. If you find that you are depending on the words of the author be skeptical. Even in the paraphrase, you must know the material well enough to put it into your own words. Phrases, turns of expression, and coined words belonging to the author must be documented.

In your search of printed materials, you may find anecdotes, interesting but little-known facts, human interest stories, and the like, that throw fresh light on what may be an all too familiar subject. Dig for these gems. The extra effort it costs you in research time to treat the subject with the spark of the unusual will pay wonderful dividends in the final paper.

DOCUMENTATION

Researched material from your People and Library files may be documented in one of three ways:

1. You may weave the information into the text, an informal way to make your reader aware of the source. Unfortunately, too many such interruptions in the flow of the text will make fearfully dull reading. But if most of the content of the work is yours with a minimum of source supports, then this method is fine:

    Dr. Colton S. Hayward wrote in his book The Cosmic Mind that . . .

    If the statement is a direct quotation by Dr. Hayward, enclose it in quotation marks. If it is paraphrased, no quotation marks are required. Remember, to paraphrase is to put another's idea into your own words, not to rearrange his words. Paraphrasing, of course, requires you to understand fully what the author is saying. The author still gets credit.

2. The second method of documenting is a little more formal. You will use numbers in the text to indicate that the material was taken from a certain source. This number is placed a half space above the typewritten line and comes *after* the source idea. It may naturally fall at the end of a sentence:

It is impossible to think in terms of success without thinking well of yourself.[1]

or it may come after each of several terms taken from different sources:

The psychology,[2] environmental pressures,[3] and philosophy[4] of the character are important in building the whole personality, for each adds to his stature[5] in the story.

Sources indicated by numbers within the text are documented in the Bibliography at the end of the paper where the information from the Bibliography is given. If you choose this second method of documentation, you may treat the Bibliography in one of three ways: (a) Alphabetize the entries and number them consecutively, corresponding to the superscript (the number following the information to be documented) in the text. (b) Enter the source material and the corresponding number in the order they appear in the text. The first time the source is entered, the complete information from the Bibliography card is given; the second time, however, short forms are used. (See the section on "Footnotes" for a full discussion of this method of documentation.) (c) If the text is long enough to be written in chapters, the sources may be given at the end of the paper, chapter by chapter, beginning at number 1 with each chapter.

3. The third method of documenting is the formal method used in all Library or Research papers. This is a more complex method, so let's review some of the steps.

Footnotes

To indicate which information in the text belongs to the source footnoted, use an Arabic number placed a half space above the typewritten line. This number is called a superscript and is placed in the text *after* the information to be documented.

At the bottom of the page, all of the information about the source that you have on your Bibliography card with the exception of the call number will be given. Form and punctuation of footnotes are important. The instructions that follow will give you the information you need to master the correct formats.

[1]Author's first name or initials, last name, <u>Title of the Book</u>, Editor or Translator if needed (Place of publication: Name of Publisher, date of publication), page or pages on which information is found.

Let's talk through the complete footnote.

Indent the same number of spaces you indent for the first line of a paragraph and give the superscript. The author's name appears next with the first name or initials followed by the last name. Comma. The title of the book, with the first letter of each significant word capitalized, is underlined. Comma. Generally, the name of the editor or translator is not needed, but if it is a book in which the editor or translator plays an important part, include the credit at this point. No punctuation. If the name of the editor or translator is not needed, then do not use any punctuation after the title of the book. Follow with a parenthesis and the place of publication. Colon. Next, the name of the publisher. Comma. Date of publication follows and the closing parenthesis. Comma. For the last item, give the page or pages for the specific information. If the reference pages are separated, use a comma between the numbers (pp. 00, 000); if they are consecutive, use a dash (pp. 000–00). Close the footnote with a period.

A footnote, without editor or translator, is written as follows:

[2]Barbara Abby, The Complete Book of Knitting (New York: The Viking Press, 1971), p. 33.

Number footnotes sequentially from page to page, making sure that the footnote is on the same page as the material it documents. When more than one footnote appears on a page, single-space individual footnotes as usual but separate references from each other by a double space.

Often, you may want to take material directly from the source. If you are using four or fewer typewritten lines, enclose the excerpt (any passage cited from the source) in quotation marks and continue with the paragraph. If, however, the excerpt is longer than four lines, set it off from the paragraph in the following manner:

> Double space after the last line of your text. Then switch to single space, as the entire excerpt is presented without extra space between lines. The left margin is indented for each line; the right margin of the excerpt, however, extends to the right margin of the text. Following the excerpt, place the superscript for the documentation that will be found in the corresponding footnote. Double space and continue with the body of the text.[3]

The different forms required for noting magazines, interviews, and so on, as well as useful short forms are illustrated at the end of this chapter.

Bibliography

A Bibliography, which is required for this method of documenting, provides a complete list of all the sources used for reference. It incorporates the same material that you entered on your Bibliography cards. Remember that you include only those sources from which you drew information for the text of your paper. If you have other sources which you did not use, don't enter them in the Bibliography.

The first line of the entry in the Bibliography is an "overhang." That is, the first line begins at the left-hand margin and the second line is indented the distance of the first line of a paragraph, the reverse of the footnote. The lines of each entry are single spaced, but the sources are separated by a double space. The following is the form for a Bibliography source:

Abbey, Barbara. <u>The Complete Book of Knitting.</u> New York:
The Viking Press, 1971.

You'll notice that the entry in the Bibliography begins with the last name of the author and then the first name. Period. (The items of the Bibliography are separated by a period.) The <u>Title of the Book,</u> underlined. Period. The place of publication. Colon. The name of the publishing company. Comma (the only comma in the entry), followed by the date. Period. No page numbers are needed. Again, make sure that you master the correct form and punctuation.

Sources are alphabetized for the Bibliography. If you have fewer than ten sources, you may place them in a single listing under the general heading "Bibliography." If, however, you have fifteen or more sources, it is better to use subheadings, separating the books (alphabetized) in one section; magazines (alphabetized) in another section; newspapers in another, and so on, all under the heading "Bibliography." Each heading should be centered. You may use either setup if your entries number between ten and fifteen.

Forms

Footnotes and Bibliography entries vary from book to magazine to encyclopedia and so on. Let's take a look at the forms you'll be using. Note that the titles of books and magazines appear in italics. These should be underlined in a typewritten paper (the underlining indicates words to be italicized in printed material). The first sample will be the footnote; the second, the Bibliography entry (*).

BOOKS

One author

[1]Bronislaw Malinowski, *Magic, Science and Religion* (Garden City, N.Y.: Doubleday Anchor Books, 1954), p. 87.

* Malinowski, Bronislaw. *Magic, Science and Religion.* Garden City, N. Y.: Doubleday Anchor Books, 1954.

One author, two or more books

[2]Will Durant, *Our Oriental Heritage* (New York: Simon and Schuster, 1954), p. 29.

[3]Will Durant, *The Story of Philosophy* (New York: Simon and Schuster, 1926), p. 90.

* Durant, Will. *Our Oriental Heritage.* New York: Simon and Schuster, 1954.

* _____. *The Story of Philosophy.* New York: Simon and Schuster, 1926.

(Note: The straight line is used in place of the author's name with the second entry.)

Two authors

[4]Robert C. Meredith and John D. Fitzgerald, *Structuring Your Novel: From Basic Idea to Finished Manuscript* (New York: Barnes and Noble Books, 1972), pp. 179–84.

* Meredith, Robert C., and John D. Fitzgerald. *Structuring Your Novel: From Basic Idea to Finished Manuscript.* New York: Barnes and Noble, 1972.

Three or more authors

[5]Marion C. Sheriden, and others, *The Motion Picture and the Teaching of English* (New York: Appleton-Century-Crofts, 1965), p. 37.

* Sheriden, Marion C., and others. *The Motion Picture and the Teaching of English.* New York: Appleton-Century-Crofts, 1965.

(Note: The Latin abbreviation *et al.* may be used instead of "and others.")

Biblical Citation

[9]I Corinthians 13:4.

(Note: Biblical and other scriptural references require no factual or publication data, although sometimes it is necessary to indicate the translation: RSV (Revised Standard Version), Jerusalem Bible, American Standard, and so on. Standard abbreviations of the names of the books in the Bible (e.g., Cor. for Corinthians) may be used. No punctuation is required except the colon between the chapter and the verse. Follow the rule of a dash between the numbers indicating continuous reading of verses and a comma between the numbers that indicate a separation. (I Corinthians 13:4, 13; or I Corinthians 13:4–13)

MAGAZINE ARTICLES

[6]S. L. A. Marshall, "The Fight at Monday," *Harper's Magazine,* November 1966, pp. 111–22.

* Marshall, S. L. A. "The Fight at Monday." *Harper's Magazine,* November 1966, pp. 111–22.

(Note: A magazine title is like a book title and must be underlined. Also notice change in punctuation.)

ENCYCLOPEDIA ARTICLES

Signed

[7]William Markowitz, "Time, Measurement and Determination Of," *Encyclopedia Americana* (1965), XXVI, 633a–33c.

* Markowitz, William. "Time, Measurement and Determination Of," *Encyclopedia Americana,* 1965, XXVI, 633a–33c.

(Note: When the volume number is given in Roman numerals without the "Vol." abbreviation, the page numbers are in Arabic without the abbreviation for page or pages.)

Unsigned

[8]"Sitting Bull," *Encyclopedia Americana* (1962), XXV, 48.

* "Sitting Bull," *Encyclopedia Americana* (1962), XXV, 48.

(Note: When the article is unsigned, use the first letter of the article title in alphabetizing the Bibliography.)

NEWSPAPERS

[10]*Wall Street Journal,* Editorial, Nov. 1, 1965, p. 8.

* *Wall Street Journal.* Editorial, Nov. 1, 1965.

INTERVIEWS

[11]Statement by Edward Teller, personal interview, July 12, 1963.

* Teller, Edward. Personal interview, July 12, 1963.

Short Forms

It would be a tedious prospect for the writer and the reader if all the information concerning the source were to be repeated each time information from the source was used in the text. Fortunately, simpler methods have been standardized and are used almost universally.

At one time, Latin abbreviations were used to indicate the second appearance and the position of the source used more than once. That meant you had to learn a list of foreign terms, understand the nuances, and meticulously dispense them according to the rules. In the economy and modernization of writing, however, the Latin terms have been dropped except for the word *ibidem* which appears in its abbreviated form as "Ibid." The use of Ibid. is the formal method of indicating ditto marks. It means that the material was found in "the same place" as the information documented above. That means that this abbreviation can be placed only directly following the source it repeats.

For instance, the first footnote of a source appears followed by the second appearance of the source.

[12]Elbert Hubbard, The Notebook of Elbert Hubbard (New York: Wm. H. Wise and Co., 1927), p. 33.

[13]Ibid.

No other footnote from another source can be placed between the first footnote and the Ibid. If the page number is different, however, you may write

[14]Ibid., p. 40.

If on one page a source is noted, followed by a second source, and the third source noted is the same as the first, you would document in the following manner:

[15]Elbert Hubbard, The Notebook of Elbert Hubbard (New York: Wm. H. Wise and Co., 1927), p. 33.

[16]Janice Freeburg, A Questionable Age of Wisdom (Las Vegas, Nevada: Barkelt and Associates, 1977), p. 40.

[17]Hubbard, p. 40.

If, however, the author has written another book that you are also using as a source, the second reference to the author would require an identification of the title in addition to the author's last name:

[18]Quotations, Hubbard, p. 90.

The same is true of magazine articles. If you are citing several articles written by the same author, in repeating references, use the title enclosed in quotation marks, the author's last name, and the page number:

[19]"Name of the Gaming," Kelley, p. 10.

3

GETTING IT TOGETHER

You've spent a good deal of time studying methods of selecting, researching, noting, and documenting material for your paper, and all that is very important, necessary work. Here you are, however, with an expansion envelope full of 3 × 5 cards covered with a wealth of information ready to be woven into an outstanding paper, and you haven't the foggiest idea what to do next.

Organize!

ORGANIZATION

You placed topics at the top-center of each notecard. Remember? Now is the time to bring together all like topics from all the sources, regardless of the file drawer you used. Sort all your notecards into separate stacks according to topic.

Let's say that you are writing about Ancient Indian Pottery in the Southwest. Suppose you have such topic headings as "kinds of clay," "designs," "etching materials," "age," and so on, and you have found something about all of these topics in most of your sources. Place all the "kinds of clay" cards together from all the sources, then place all the "design" cards together, and continue sorting until all the cards have been placed in their proper stack. This is your first step in organizing the mass of material you have researched.

Leave your cards for a moment and go back to the Statement of Purpose.

Read the Statement of Purpose and study the Controlling Idea. Determine three strong Main Points that will support or prove the Controlling Idea. Write down the points, each on a separate card. Spread these cards out on the table in front of you. Now, go through the notecards and select the topics you think best support the three points, placing the supporting topic cards under the Main Point card to which they belong. Do not shoehorn a piece of information into the supporting material. If the information isn't pertinent to one of the Main Points and the Controlling Idea, put it aside for the time being. Caution: Don't throw away any card until you have completed the paper as you may have use for it later on.

Some cards will be left over. Study them to see if some of the material belongs in the Beginning or Introduction of the paper. If so, place those notecards beneath another card titled Beginning. Others of the cards may be conclusive in their information. If so, place them in another stack marked Ending. Again, don't shoehorn. Don't worry if cards are left over, for you'll have use for them later.

At this point, you should have five stacks of cards:

Beginning
    1. Introduction
Middle
    2. Main Point #1
    3. Main Point #2
    4. Main Point #3
Ending
    5. Conclusion

It is well to remember that we are discussing the shorter paper, one within the 2,000 to 3,000 word limit, as it is in this range that most assigned papers fall. For this length paper, you must have three Main Points. If you have fewer than three, your Statement of Purpose may fizzle for lack of support. If you have more than three, chances are you haven't studied your material closely enough and are trying to handle too much information. If the assignment is for a paper of greater length, you may have as many as five points, but no more.

Now, this does not mean that you will have only five paragraphs in the paper. The support topics you have selected may indicate that several paragraphs are required to satisfactorily present one Main Point. However, if you extend your supports into several paragraphs for one Main Point, do so for the others also, in order to create a balance in your writing.

The next step in the organization process is to arrange the support cards in their proper order. What is the most effective way of presenting your information? How does the sequence of information best lead to a conclusion of the point? Work with the placement of the cards until you feel the information moves smoothly from one idea to another.

EVALUATION

Check each of the support cards against the Statement of Purpose:

- Does this thought point directly to and support the Controlling Idea?
- Does this idea help clarify the Controlling Idea?
- Does each of the supporting ideas truly support or prove the Main Point it belongs to?
- Does this support in fact detour from the idea the Main Point is trying to prove?

Again, it is important to remember that at this stage of your writing you can't afford to throw away any of your cards, so if one appears to be alien, put it aside for later consideration. What you think may be useless information now may be just the idea you will need later.

After you complete your evaluation, you are ready to begin your Outline.

OUTLINE

Outlining is the area where most writers bog down.

In the past, you've worked out an outline for your subject in the formal Roman-numeral manner:

> I.
>> A.
>>> 1.
>>> 2.
>> B.
>>> 1.
>>> 2.
> II.
>> And so on . . .

Suddenly, you find that III-B should appear in the place of II-C and II-C should be moved to VI-D-1. Great! Now you have to rewrite the whole outline in order to reorganize.

With notecards, this time-consuming process is not necessary. Cards are quite "mobile" and can be easily arranged and rearranged without any writing. In minutes, you can make major changes, subtle changes, any changes that are needed to make the paper tight and well organized, simply by moving the cards until you have the most effective place for the information. You can work with the cards until you settle on the outline that seems best, and at no time do you have to write a word.

Let's see how this works.

Spread the five stacks of cards in front of you: Beginning, Main Points #1, #2, #3, and Ending. As you study the cards, try to visualize the completed paper. Is the idea stated clearly in the Beginning? Does the thought run through each Main Point of the Middle and conclude quite naturally in the Ending? You are still working with the raw material on the cards, not the finished product, but your overview of the paper should be clear enough for you to picture the effectiveness of the paper.

When you are satisfied that your outline is the best you can arrange, clip together the cards that will comprise each paragraph and place them under the Main Point they support. Put a rubber band around each division.

Once you have carefully completed these steps, you are ready for the easy part of the work: writing. It isn't difficult to make a trip once the itinerary is set and all the preparations completed. You have no outline to copy, no supplementary material to consult. You'll work directly from the cards that you have carefully arranged in the proper order, grouped into paragraphs, and placed in the sections where they belong. You will begin with the first card, write, go to the second, and so on, until you have all your thoughts and material on paper. The next chapter will tell you how.

4

WRITING

Basically, all writing is reduced to three main sections:

- Beginning
- Middle
- Ending

This is the basic pattern of books (fiction or nonfiction), articles, papers of all kinds, and letters. It is the basis for speeches and most kinds of public communication.

BASIC SECTIONS OF A PAPER

The length and content of each main section will vary according to the kind of writing you are doing and the requirements of the specific paper. A novel, for instance, may have a Beginning that continues for several chapters, since the body of the story doesn't usually begin until the protagonist makes a clearcut decision to act upon his problem. Nonfiction books seldom take that much space for the Beginning but rather inform the reader at the outset of the purpose of the work.

Sometimes changes in the arrangement of your outline will

be indicated in the requirements for individual papers, but having studied and mastered this method of outlining, you will be flexible enough in your thinking to apply the method to any of the papers you'll ever be required to write. Let's look again at the outline.

    I. Beginning
        A. Hook opening
        B. Beginning
   II. Middle
        A. Main Point #1
            1. Supporting idea
            2. Supporting idea
        B. Main Point #2
            1. Supporting idea
            2. Supporting idea
        C. Main Point #3
            1. Supporting idea
            2. Supporting idea
  III. Ending

Opening

In going through your cards, you may have come across a story, an anecdote, a quotation, something that is bound to "hook" your reader's attention and draw him into the rest of the paper. You may want to use a statement of such interest that the reader feels compelled to read the paper to satisfy his curiosity. Be sure that this opening paragraph is pertinent to the theme of the paper. You won't want to tell a story that has nothing to do with the subject of the paper. Readers lose interest in the paper and confidence in you as a writer if you plant a false trail that leads away from the matter to be discussed. No tricks! If you use a hook, it should appear in a paragraph prior to the Beginning paragraph.

Beginning

If you plan to start with the Beginning paragraph, let your first sentence be provocative. Catch the reader's attention. Broadly touch upon the subject and let each following sentence narrow in scope until you give the reader the Statement of Purpose. Don't copy the Statement of Purpose that guided you this far. Rewrite it. In the rewording, however, make sure you remain true to the Controlling Idea.

This Beginning sets the mood (serious, amusing, informative, scholarly) and gives the slant the paper will take. It indicates what you intend to cover in the Middle, or body, of the paper. It is your promise to the reader. Again, don't try to fool the reader as to the direction you are taking. You know your Controlling Idea; let the reader know it too. (Exceptions to the treatment of the Beginning paragraph will be covered in Part II in the discussion of specific types of papers.)

Ending

Now it's time to write the Ending of the paper. Before writing the Middle? you ask. Yes, before writing the Middle! You have a good, strong first paragraph, and you'll need an equally strong closing one. You're not tired or rushed to complete the paper. Think how comforting it will be to know while you're writing the Middle that the Ending is completed.

Take a note from the highly successful adage of old show business. Years ago, Balban and Katz, theater men of Chicago, built their shows on the premise that if you give the audience a strong opening and a strong closing, the middle takes care of itself. That isn't entirely true, and they knew it, for the Middle is also worthy of one's best. But no matter how grand the performance, if the closing is weak because you're tired of the whole project the audience goes away dissatisfied. That is true with the paper. If the Beginning is attention getting and the

Ending is a rousing conclusion à la Balban and Katz, the reader closes the paper with an appreciation of the whole "show."

The first step will be to reword the Statement of Purpose so that it can be woven into the text of the final paragraph. You'll notice that this is a second rewording, not a copy of the Statement of Purpose or of the reworded Statement in the first paragraph. This is a referral to the Beginning, a reminder of the Controlling Idea your entire paper supports.

From this point, ease into broader and broader statements until you have concluded your discussion. A carefully planned paper can be satisfactorily concluded in one paragraph. If you study your material closely and "listen" to the logical progression of your discussion, you'll find the material will point the way to an effective conclusion.

The Ending may be in the form of a summary, but care must be taken not to make the reader feel that you doubt his ability to understand the paper at the first reading and so must have it reviewed for him. Touch briefly on a generalized summation of the subject.

You may prefer to introduce new material instead of using the summary. Again, care must be taken that the new material is pertinent and does not suggest a detour or open further discussion of the subject.

If, for example, you have discussed a medical problem, you may want to use a promissory ending, one that gives hope. You may conclude with a quotation that strikes a desired effect, or you may like to close with an anecdote that conclusively points to the purpose of the paper.

Whatever type of Ending you decide to use, the important thing is that you give the article a satisfactory note of finality.

Middle

The Middle or body of the paper contains the strength of the argument, the bulk of the information you are offering. This section will be longer than either of the other two sections of the paper, for here you will build to a climax the topics you've selected to support your Controlling Idea. In turn, you will arrange the sequence of the minor supports so that they, too, will move smoothly and directly toward the conclusion of your argument. First, let's take a closer look at the outline of the Middle section:

A. Main Point #1 (support of Controlling Idea)
  1. minor support
  2. minor support
B. Main Point #2
  1. minor support
  2. minor support
C. Main Point #3
  1. minor support
  2. minor support

Each of the Main Points could easily be a paragraph, giving you a five-paragraph paper. You may have sufficient material, however, to comfortably flesh out the Main Points and related minor supports into multiple paragraphs, and thus create a longer paper. Make your plans before you begin writing.

Whichever approach you decide on, always remember to save your strongest support for last, as this type of buildup will create the biggest impact on the reader.

INTEREST

We've talked about finding "interesting" things to write about, and writing "interestingly," but what are some of the tools that will help you write in an "interesting" manner?

Dialogue. Our attention is drawn to conversation. Though we are not always eavesdropping, we are beings with curiosity. We like to hear the turn of phrase that makes one person's speech different from another's. We enjoy the characteristic lilt and life of the exchange of talk. True, we do like to investigate exposition, too, but nothing sparks up the encounter like lively dialogue.

In writing and reading, the same thing occurs. So much can be put into dialogue to advance the paper, to give us a glimpse of the speaker, to draw our attention. Dialogue also breaks up the paragraphing, thus creating additional visual interest on the page.

Try to make the dialogue sound as lifelike as possible. In speech, we are inclined to use a verbal shorthand in which much of the meaning is derived from inflection, gesture, and the background of the person with whom we are speaking. In writing, we have to put the inflection, the gesture, the back-ground into the dialogue and still be true to the personality of the speaker.

It isn't as hard as it sounds. Write your dialogue as you think the individual speaks, then read it aloud. You'll be amazed at how hearing what you've written, even in your own voice, will remind you of certain words the speaker uses and other man-nerisms of speech unique to him.

Authority. Chances are good that you are not an authority on your subject. You may know a great deal about it, but you haven't been acclaimed by your peers or the country. There-fore, you will need the words of an authority on the subject to underscore what you have to say. The library will provide you with plenty of information in this category. What do some of the "big" people in the field say about your subject? Do any of these experts live near you? An interview would be excellent.

Facts. Nothing carries the weight that facts do when it comes to proving a point. How, the reader says, can I argue with the facts? A fact is something that has been proven to be true; something that is infallible; something that can be verified.

However, facts can be tricky. Take care that you do a thorough job in gathering them. Check to make sure that they provide the strongest possible support for your Controlling Idea. And be accurate. An incorrect fact is no fact at all. It is wise to verify your facts in one or more additional sources, as "authorities" sometimes disagree. Also, check to be sure you haven't distorted the meaning of your facts by citing them out of context.

Anecdotes.   An anecdote is a short narrative or story that illustrates your Controlling Idea. It must directly support the idea, for it is told for that reason, not merely for the sake of telling a story. Sometimes the anecdote is a true story, but often it is a piece of fiction composed for the express purpose of illustrating the point you are making.

Quotations.   What famous person has something to say about your subject? What does an expert say? What does a layman say? To quote someone on the subject, particularly someone important to the subject, is to lend further authority to the paper. Quote accurately, being careful not to change the speaker's viewpoint. Enclose the quotation in quotation marks, and make sure to identify and document the source.

Illustrations.   An illustration is a narrative example that supports the Controlling Idea. It explains something that has happened or is happening in the subject field.

Facts give objective details; illustrations show people doing things. Anecdotes provide relevant stories; illustrations relate events that prove the point you are trying to make.

You may use any one of these tools for interest in writing your paper, or you may use several. Take care, however, that you don't sprinkle them obviously throughout your writing. When you use one, work it smoothly into your paper so that it becomes a part of the whole piece.

FIRST DRAFT

The first draft is your first opportunity to bring together all the material you have gathered in a written out form. Your card outline is your guide, your mind-jogger, that will keep you *on* the main line and *off* the detours you may be tempted to investigate along the way. By following the method of preparation presented in this book, you will be forced to use your own words, and therefore you will write a fresher, more spontaneous paper.

Write the entire paper at one sitting if you can. If not, try to end your writing periods at the completion of one step of the outline. Remember to double space everything you write so that you will have room to enter notes or corrections.

Don't rewrite any more than you must; but do rewrite as often as you must. Just what does that say?

Some people are perfectionists and never feel satisfied with their work. As a result, they write and rewrite, not realizing that they have done the best they can at this stage of their learning. In such cases, it is foolish to keep working on an assignment. You must know that you will grow with each paper and that your level of writing will be higher with each guided effort.

The reverse is true of others. They are satisfied as soon as they have written a sufficient number of words to complete the assignment and feel that a rewrite is entirely unnecessary. Ridiculous! A first draft is *never* ready to be turned in as final copy. If professionals use the proofread-rewrite method, beginners most certainly should too.

REVISING

Read over what you have written. You will do well to read it aloud because this will force you to read slowly enough to study the sense of your writing. Have you clearly presented your thoughts to the reader? Have you logically supported your Controlling Idea, the point you promised to get across? Have you padded, inserting words and sentences that could be deleted without harming the text? Have you used twenty-five words to write a sentence when ten would do; fifty when twenty-five would have been better?

Now is the time for you to make your deletions, check on transitions, smooth the continuity, polish the style, correct spelling and punctuation. Rewrite portions if you think it is necessary, or all of it if you honestly think you can do a better job.

At this step, you will find that scissors and a paste pot will help considerably. You can always cross out unnecessary words or sentences, but rewriting paragraphs directly on the first draft gets messy and cramped and only confuses your flow of thought. You'll end up with a rewritten page that is too short, which you'll madly try to stretch. You'll find a paragraph that is too long, and you may feel driven to reword sentences while you are typing. Somehow, you never seem to catch up on the spacing. Instead, write the revised paragraph on another piece of paper and paste it over the first try. If the rewrite is longer than the original, simply cut out the first and insert the second. What difference does it make if the pages vary in length? This is a working copy.

Check again for capitalization, spelling, punctuation. Check for clarity. You know what you proposed to say. Did you say it?

FINAL COPY

The final step in preparing your manuscript for class, for market, or for whatever other purpose, is a professional method of presentation. Don't be a nonconformist in this particular area. You've outgrown the scrapbook stage and the fancy colored-paper stage. From now on you will present your material as formally and as professionally as you can. Follow each step carefully:

1. Use standard 8½ × 11-inch typing paper. Use only white paper.

   If you are preparing the paper to submit to a publisher, use 20-pound white bond paper.

2. Use only one side of the paper. Never type or write on both sides of a page.

3. Type neatly. If you must handwrite, be sure that your writing is entirely legible—but you better check ahead of time. If typewritten copy is required, you may have to hire someone to type it for you.

   If a publisher is going to see this paper, type it.

4. Double space your copy, whether it is typed or handwritten.

5. For a class assignment, write on the first page, your name, class, teacher, and date in the upper left-hand corner. In the upper right-hand corner, place the number or name of the assignment.

   If you plan to market your short piece, place your name and address in the extreme upper left-hand corner and the approximate number of words in the upper right-hand corner.

   In either case, place the title of the piece about 22 spaces down from the top and center it. Then skip down 8 spaces and begin the text of your paper.

   Number the first page 4 spaces up from the bottom of the page and center.

   See Figure 6.

6. On the second and following pages, place only your name in the upper left-hand corner of the page. In the upper right-hand corner, place the page number. Use Arabic numbers and let them stand alone—no dashes on either side or period following.

```
Name                              Name of Assignment
Class
Teacher
Date

                    22 spaces




                Title of Paper

                  9 spaces



        Begin the text at this point.   Indent the first line

of each paragraph, double space, and leave 1 1/2-inch

margins on the top, bottom, left, and right, unless the

paper is to be bound (in which case, leave a 2-inch margin

on the left).
```

Figure 6.   First page of paper

If the piece is to be submitted for publication, it is wise to include the title on each page. If the title is long, use only an identifying portion of it. Center the page number and, on the same level, place the full or shortened title in the upper right-hand corner.

7. Leave a 1½-inch margin on each side of the page unless the paper is to be bound, in which case, leave a 2-inch margin on the left side. Again, if the teacher has stated any preferences, follow his instructions.

8. Don't ever hand in a dog-eared paper or a paper with smudges and unnecessary marks on it.

9. All papers should be handed in flat unless you are otherwise instructed. You may staple or clip the pages together or place them in a binder. Again follow the instructions of the teacher. *Never* fold and tear the corner of the paper in an effort to fasten.

   If the paper is to go to an editor, keep the pages flat and loose. Do not staple, clip, or bind the sheets. The one exception is the short-short piece of fewer than five pages. These you may fold once and send in an envelope to fit. (You may support the pages in the envelope when sending them flat by including a thin piece of cardboard the size of the pages.)

10. When submitting a piece for publication, always be sure to enclose an SASE (a self-addressed stamped envelope) and make sure you have included sufficient postage for the possible return of your piece. Do not attach the stamps, but fasten them to the enclosed envelope with a clip.

PART TWO
...ANYTHING

5

TYPES OF PAPERS

You may be asked to write one of many types of papers. Although the writing process is basically the same for all of them, it is important to learn the personality of each type of paper, its requirements, and its outline.

The following sections analyze the various types of papers. Some are informal and typical of those published in newspapers and magazines; others are formal and typical of the papers required for college courses. All of them incorporate the techniques discussed in the previous section. Your competence will be demonstrated in your ability to apply these techniques to specific types of papers. Develop paragraphs carefully, write effective sentences, and use words worthy of the time and effort you will spend in writing the paper.

Everything you write reflects a bit of you, the author. You will want to take care to put your "best foot forward," to show yourself at advantage. This means that you will use good taste —that elusive standard set by the majority as representative of humanity at its best. You will use correct English, choosing the level according to the formality or informality of the paper. Make sure, however, that you don't fall below standard English except for such dialogue as you may introduce because of its pertinence to the subject. If there is a taboo in writing, it concerns the use of idioms or colloquialisms, not because they are wrong, but because in a cross-section of readers, too few would be familiar with the expressions.

If, in the following study of the individual types of papers, you find that information is repeated, know that it is important enough to warrant repeating. It is easy to forget, and a reminder within the framework of the discussion is often helpful. Models of the papers are not given, for the intent is to outline and then flesh out the process so that you, uninhibited by a set model, can see the growth of your own paper and sense your achievement.

EXPERIENCE

Experience papers will probably be the first types of paper you are asked to write. It is the least complex type, for the material all comes from your Memory file. You don't have to go to the library to research your topic nor do you have to interview people to gather material. The experience paper describes events in the order of their happening, that is, chronologically. Make no pretense of explaining or proving anything; simply re-create the experience and enjoy it.

First, choose an experience that will be interesting in the telling and then tell it with all the excitement and interest you can recall; express it colorfully, and your readers will be interested, too. This paper need not be one of the old chestnuts—what I did last summer, a narrow escape, or an embarrassing moment—although cleverly written, any of these would make good reading.

You might tell about the time you won the jackpot on a dollar slot machine in Las Vegas. It could be a race-car show that you visited, training for the Olympics, your first trip to Paris, a religious experience. This is not a how-to approach, but a narrative about an experience you had in a specific area of your life. Your interest is in recounting the "doing" of the experience, and is not necessarily about you. This keeps you from feeling embarrassment about recounting events of your life; yet the reader must feel that you were there all the time.

Go through the process of making cards on all the things you can remember about your subject. What did people wear? What was the location? What was going on generally? Specifically, what was happening? How about the weather? What time of day, or year, did it happen? What were the circumstances? Everything you can remember, you must put on a card as you learned to do in Chapter 1.

Once you have "pulled" everything about the subject from your memory, write the Statement of Purpose and underline the Controlling Idea. You are not expected to come up with some abstract, profound idea. You are entertaining the reader by sharing with him this event in your life. Then arrange the cards in sequence.

Experience papers are written in narrative form, moving chronologically. They are usually written in the first person, giving them that warm, I-was-there quality that readers enjoy. Unless you are an expert writer, to put the experience in the third person would give your paper a brittle, phony atmosphere. Therefore, your point of view will be first person. Take care, however, that you don't clutter the paper with *I*'s. Did you ever check over a personal letter you've just written? Chances are the *I*'s stand out like telephone poles because you are reporting on your very own personal activities; *I* is the main character of what you are saying. With a little effort when writing an Experience paper, you can maintain the same warm, personal touch, and still not have the page bristle with *I*.

The second person is seldom used throughout a paper. It sounds preachy or teachy to continually refer to *you*. Sometimes when relating your experience in the first person becomes a bit embarrassing, *you* is a pleasant shift for the writer, but try to be objective and selective in using it.

Write simply, allowing the length of the sentences to follow the pace of the story—the rush of excitement, the peace of a pastoral scene, the chop of rugged action. How is this done? By matching your words to the subject material. Try telling the story of a fight in long, liquid sentences. It doesn't come off too well, does it? Fight pictures are created by short, clipped sentences and hard-hitting words. Thoughtful pictures need longer, more flowing sentences. Ideally, both types of descriptions should have variations in sentence length.

Beginning

The Beginning of the Experience paper is typical of all Beginnings for here you capture the reader's attention and introduce your Purpose. With your card outline before you, you have a sketch of the overall picture you want to paint. Spend time creating the most interesting introduction possible. Establish your place, the people involved, and a promise of the action.

The Experience paper is an informal narrative, so be chatty in your writing. Most Experience papers move along at a lively tempo. To keep the story moving, use vivid verbs and few adjectives, employ sentence variety, and keep your paragraphs fairly short. You can dispense with *to be* verbs unless it is absolutely impossible to write the sentence without them. Also, try not to use the passive voice:

The bear was hit by Bob.

So what? Your aim is to bring an experience to life, so you want to show action. Therefore, use the active voice:

Bob hit the bear.

Now, that is a much more exciting happening and promises the reader some activity as a result.

Middle

As soon as you have established the subject, mood, and something of the environment, begin the story. The Middle, remember, is the strength of your paper. Let the interest heighten as you move toward the climax or peak of your story. This peak is the culmination of your Statement of Purpose and leads to the conclusion.

To help you "show" the things that happened, borrow from the fiction writer's bag of tricks. Use narration, dialogue, description, an occasional flashback, tension. All these add color to your writing.

Narration. In using narration, you may tell about typical events, things that happen habitually, to establish the circumstances: "Dad always took over for backyard cooking," "Elsa always managed to say the wrong thing," "Monday, as usual, was a day of blahs!" It may be that you will want to cover less important events not worthy of detailed recounting but necessary for the story. This you may do by summarizing such events, touching on them but not detailing them.

Finally, you will want to tell the dramatic, step-by-step action of the experience by giving the reader direct scenes. Show! Let the reader see what happened. The dramatized narrative is the complete picture including dialogue, action, description, and so on. In it you will *show* the action.

Dialogue. Dialogue keeps the story alive, especially if you have your characters speak as they really do in life. Each person has a different speech pattern. Listen to your friends. Or better yet, tape conversations and then listen to them. You can pick out the individuals not only by the sounds of their voices but also by the patterns of their speech. You must learn to achieve the same effect with the dialogue in your papers. However, one caution: Do not use dialogue simply to spark the looks of the paper or to break up the line of paragraphs. If the dialogue does not advance the development of your story, leave it out.

Once you've written a dialogue, it's a good idea to read it aloud so that you can judge whether or not the sound is natural or phony, informative or merely passing the time of day. Use only dialogue that forwards or enhances what you are writing.

Flashback.   Although the Experience paper progresses in a chronological manner, you may occasionally find that a "flashback" to an earlier episode makes the telling easier and heightens interest more than if the same information is put in its correct chronological sequence. Much of this depends on where you began your narrative. As in a short story, the Experience paper begins chronologically as close to the climax, or the punch line, as feasible; therefore, from time to time you may want to draw in a bit of exposition to clarify an event.

If you do use a flashback, make sure that it is clear to the reader that you are taking him back in time. The shift should be easy and should seem entirely natural. You might introduce the flashback with "Once, I remember, Dad . . ." or "That was when Jack . . ." or "Earlier, Louise left for . . ."

Description.   Description is the tool you use to paint a word picture and is helpful in all your papers. You may want to re-create a beautiful scene for your reader; you may want to share the sounds and sights of a police action you witnessed; you may want to set a mood. Again, a caution: Do not stop the movement of the narrative to describe a scene you are particularly fond of unless it is important to the story.

Impressions of the senses are an important element in writing description. What can you smell? Jasmine from a Persian garden; new-cut alfalfa; warm milk; freshly baked bread; a heady perfume; dust; rain?

What do you feel? The cold of metal; the soft of fur; the grit of sand; the squish of mud; the warmth of flesh; the press of welcome?

What do you hear? A slide; a scream; a muffled step; a whisper; a sniffle; a gasp; a laugh?

What do you taste? Salty tears; the acid of fear; sweet-sour; the tart of citrus; barbecue steaks; apple pie?

What do you see? A cluttered room; a pastoral scene; a busy train station; a crippled woman; an old man with a cane; a frosty glass of iced tea; a birthday cake; a sleeping baby?

By describing the impressions of the senses, you can transport your reader into any situation you care to conjure for him. Much of the power of writing comes from the skillful use of this tool, for even in How-to papers, reminders of sense-awareness will improve interest.

Figures of speech help to make descriptive writing more vivid, but beware of clichés. Try a simile. A simile is a comparison of unlike things introduced by the use of "like" and "as":

> His wallet was as flat as a pizza.

> She looked like a puppy left out in the rain.

Perhaps a metaphor is your choice of comparing unlikes. A metaphor is an implied comparison and is expressed without "like" or "as":

> A lacy veil of leaves and branches shaded the path.

> The street was a steaming mush of melting snow.

Interesting writing often results from the use of personification, a figure of speech in which the writer attributes human characteristics to animals, objects, or ideas.

> The old house scolded the newfangled cars that dared to park in front of her.

Be careful of overwriting figures of speech. Many young writers gush with expressions such as "silver, shimmering pools of fragrance hung on the sweetly scented atmosphere of love." You can easily drip-dry sentences by overwriting.

Beware of adjectives. A string of adjectives can weaken any scene you write regardless of the picture you are painting. Instead of tacking adjectives onto the nouns, try using vivid verbs or an occasional appositive. You will be pleased at the spark your writing will have.

To hold together the details of a descriptive paragraph, try using adverbs of place such as *next, beyond,* and *this.* (Look for others to use.)

A general impression may help to unify the description:

> The room looked like a storeroom in a bargain basement. Clothes were on every available seat, and Jim's mackinaw, gloves, and snowshoes covered the top of his unmade bed.

To give the reader a scene as vivid as that picture in your mind, you must be able to see it in great detail. From your mental picture, work out a pattern: left to right, right to left, up-down, down-up.

At no time allow dialogue, flashbacks, or description to stop the forward movement of the story. Weave them into the paper so that the reader feels a constant movement toward the climax of the event.

Ending

As is common to all papers, Ending of the Experience paper must conclude the story. It may require a paragraph to tie up loose ends or it may conclude in a single sentence. Just remember that once you have delivered the punch line—accomplished your purpose—you have little else to tell.

Probably the most effective ending is a referral to the first paragraph which allows you to restate the Controlling Idea. Or you might conclude by leaving the reader with a descriptive detail. Make sure, whatever type of conclusion you choose, that you end the paper with finality.

PRÉCIS

In school and in everyday work, you will often find yourself in the position of having to write a brief, accurate summary of an article, an occasion, a speech. This summary report may be prepared for your own files, for others to read, or for presentation to a group. Therefore, it must be accurate and concise.

This brief summary is called a Précis, a French word pronounced /prā′-sē/. The spelling is the same for singular and plural, with the plural being pronounced with a final /z/ sound /prā′-sēz/.

The purpose of the Précis is to get to the heart or core of the material on which you are reporting, be it a book, magazine article, discussion, conversation, newspaper account, or meeting. To do this, you will have to study the material until you know the purpose behind it. Only when the meaning is clear in your mind will you be able to convey the pertinent, essential ideas, the attitudes and emphasis, the tone embedded in the original.

Great care must be made to maintain the author's point of view, for although the précis is written in your own words, you must not express your opinions or add your personal coloring to the subject. However, you will select colorful words (this does not mean coloring the author's thoughts) that show action or emphasize the author's precise thoughts.

Don't be caught in the paraphrase trap. A paraphrase is merely saying the same thing in a different and simpler manner and often requires more words than the original. Furthermore, at no time are you allowed to copy anything the author said, even if you dutifully give him credit; nor can you refer to

him or his work, as indicated by "The author says . . ." or
"This paragraph means . . ." The reader knows that you are
reporting the author's thoughts and from your accurate accounting he will make his own assessments of the author's
meaning.

Choose your words carefully, economically, using them skillfully to get the maximum meaning in the minimum number of
words. How long, then, can a Précis be?

You may reduce the material to a quarter of the length of the
original if in cutting you are careful not to shortchange the
author's purpose. The important thing is to focus on the core
idea of the material and write clearly and without distortion the
gist of the whole article.

It is quite possible that a single sentence is sufficient for an
average paragraph of original material. In fact, a single sentence carefully structured may reflect the thought of several
paragraphs, for if you remember, a writer may use several paragraphs of minor supports to explain and uphold one Main Point
of his article. All the information in these supporting paragraphs falls under the Main Point. Therefore, if you discover the
Main Points of the material at hand, you will be able to briefly
summarize in your own words the purpose of the article, using
only such minor details as you need to flesh out the summary
smoothly and sensibly. Keep it short, well within a third the
length of the original.

The main points that you must consider when writing a Précis are:

- Get to the heart of the material
- Maintain the author's point of view
- Add no personal opinion or color
- Do not paraphrase
- Use your own words
- Move in the same order chosen by the author
- Write one-third or less the length of the original

PROFILE

A Profile is a concise character sketch, often a one-trait story, that is vividly written to tell what an individual's distinctive trait or ability is. As a sort of informal biography, it snoops into some secret corners and informs the reader of a person who would be interesting to know. We learn a little about his immediate family, maybe something of his friends, and how his trait or ability got him in and out of the experiences that filled his life.

A Profile requires rather extensive knowledge of the subject, which means more than a trip to the library or the newspaper morgue. To find the human interest touches that color the picture, you need to talk with friends, relatives, employers, competitors. Know as much about your subject as you can. If possible, arrange an interview so that you can hear his voice, observe his mannerisms, catch his smile. An interview is also a way to learn something of his interest in his own life.

Take notes during the discussion. Try to catch everything so that when you begin writing your material will be so rich that you will have to skillfully select the incidents you can use.

Beginning

Your first paragraph should give the reader a picture of the subject. He may be talking about himself, discussing the trait that made him famous—or infamous. He may be at work in an art studio or playing a musical instrument. You may show him at a drafting board, in a greenhouse, or accepting the winner's flag at a car race. Don't weigh the reader down with description, but show enough of the subject so that the reader will feel as if he has met and talked with the person himself.

Middle

The second and following paragraphs in the middle of the paper touch upon the biography of the individual, informing the reader of his family, his friends, and his working environment. The paper is written in narrative form and moves best chronologically. Your first paragraph, the Beginning, is a current picture, the way he looks now. Your second paragraph, which starts the Middle section, should begin at the time when his trait or ability was first evidenced. Starting at that point, weave into the story something of his personality, his appearance, his mannerisms. Show his growing skill. Show his acceptance by others in the field and by the public. Continue by dealing with the high spots of the subject's life bringing the information up to date. Let us, the readers, see him, watch him at work, laugh with him.

Ending

The Ending is a continuation of the current picture of the subject. In your final paragraph you may want to return to the scene you set up in your opening paragraph and continue with it. Let the subject tell you something of his plans, the promise he feels the future holds for him.

You may want your final paragraph to show the subject in another contemporary scene, different from the first but still showing his ability and skill. Again, let him tell of the picture he holds for his future. When you conclude the paper, the reader should feel that he has made a new friend.

Profile of Yourself

If you are asked to write something about yourself for a teacher or a potential employer, follow the outline of the Profile, with yourself as subject. It is difficult to be the subject of your own paper, but try to be objective in selecting interesting experiences or positions you have held that support the purpose of your writing. If the Profile is required for a job application, then concern yourself with your professional experiences. Show the potential employer positions you've held or training and experience you've had in the field. If the Profile is for school, focus on abilities, skills, training, and so on, that direct the teacher's attention toward your goals. Show what you have done that indicates you are proficient in the field as far as you have gone. You can follow the Profile outline and adapt your traits and abilities to it.

This outline is also excellent for the brief biography you may be asked to send in with your application for a scholarship.

Be careful about padding the paper with inconsequentials. For instance, you were obviously born or you wouldn't be writing the self-profile. It is unnecessary to explain to the reader that "I was born June . . . " Similarly, it is unnecessary to explain that you were born of "poor but honest," "hard-working," or "God-fearing" parents. Of course, if your parents have some special, out-of-the-ordinary characteristic, then an explanation of this fact in great detail is a must—providing it helps you clarify the reason for your proficiency in your field.

Treat yourself as objectively as possible, holding back on the use of the personal pronoun. You'll do a fine job. Be sure to keep a copy of your personal Profile in your files. You never know when you may need it or want to use it as a model for other Profile papers.

HOW-TO

The world is filled with people with How-to-do-itis. They buy kits and follow directions on how to construct everything from model airplanes to pipe organs. On the premise that they need

to know how to assemble the kits or use the appliances, manu-
facturers have tagged each item with instructions. Clothes have
tickets explaining how the garment is to be washed. In fact,
scientists hand over their findings to writers who are charged
with explaining the material in layman's terms.

The range of How-to writing runs from the extremely formal
paper, intended primarily or exclusively for the reader who
already knows something about the subject, to the very simple
instructions for the youngster who wants a guide to help him
complete a kit all by himself.

You must understand the subject before you can write such
a paper, for the difficulty in the How-to paper is being able to
identify the progression of the steps and clearly instruct the
reader so that he moves in a straight line from the beginning
to the end. How can you explain to a student how to play a
diatonic scale on the piano if you don't thoroughly understand
the process yourself? Often, however, it is simple to do something, but very difficult to explain the process to someone else.

The tone of the How-to paper need not be coldly factual. Use
your own descriptive manner of saying things; just remain honest and accurate. Interpret if you wish and express an occasional
opinion, but make sure that you keep these personal touches
incidental to the information.

Beginning

The Beginning serves only to introduce the subject, to interest the how-to-doer so that he will be glad he chose the project.
Introduce the subject in your own words and describe the
finished product in order to acquaint the reader with his goal.
This description should heighten the reader's interest.

Middle

The Middle is the important part of the paper. Here you
give a step-by-step description of what is to be done. Explain

the details of the process and describe the tricks of the trade that will make the work easier. An accurately identified diagram or sketch is a helpful aid as it provides the reader an opportunity to check his own work. Offer encouragement by describing accomplishments as you and the reader progress. However, although the writing should be interesting, always keep in mind that clarity is the most important element of the How-to paper.

Ending

The Ending shows, very briefly, what the reader has made by following your instructions. Step by step he has constructed the item. Close, now, with a slap on the back for the how-to-doer. End with an anecdote or a pertinent quotation that will leave the reader with a smile on his face. Or perhaps you have other suggestions you'd like to share for how he can use the item he has made. Don't stretch to be the comic. Just keep things pleasant.

PROCESS

The How-to outline may also be used when writing a Process paper, a particular kind of information paper that emphasizes *how* and *what*. In this paper, you'll describe the operation of a machine, the performing of a scientific experiment, how a philosophy may be learned and used, how a goal is accomplished. You'll notice, however, that although the Process paper is a form of the How-to paper, it is not limited to the step-by-step method found in many technical papers.

Beginning

Identify the process, whether it relates to a mechanical device or falls into the mental or self-help category. Define terms and explain techniques and equipment. In the Beginning, let the reader know what is in store for him.

Middle

The Middle of the Process paper describes the mechanism or activity. It shows how the goal can be accomplished and encourages the reader to strive to achieve it. When writing this type of paper, refer back to the section on "Interest" (pages 48–50). Use some of these "tools" to give life to your writing. How others accomplished the goal of this process is important, so include one or two such cases. The reader learns from these illustrations that others have been in the same position in which he finds himself, and sees what processes they followed to overcome the situation. The reader can learn how scientific discoveries are made, how new and complex machines function.

Ending

The Ending of the Process paper is the achievement of the goal, the purpose of the whole process. Once this high point is reached, there is really nothing more to say. Why not end with an anecdote or a quotation? Challenge the reader so that he will want to study other processes in the same field. Again, the Purpose must be finalized in the last sentence or paragraph.

OPINION

"Opinion! Great! Now I can tell them what I think."

True! However, every paper in the writing game has a few ground rules, and the Opinion paper is no exception. The first thing a writer must recognize is that the other fellow has as much right to his opinion as you have to yours. There's no way you can persuade another person to see things your way if you blast him with your superiority and point out his incompetency to think straight. Give your reader credit for intelligence, for judgment, for arriving at the point where he has formed an opinion just as you have. Then you may ask him to consider your side of the subject.

What is an opinion? It is a conclusion you reach after you have analyzed and weighed all your research on the subject: your interviews, your reading, your own experience. It is the result of carefully studying both sides of the subject. Your judgment is based on the weight of the evidence you have uncovered. To do less is to work with prejudices. Regardless of how many authorities you have consulted on the subject, you must understand that, in the final analysis, the opinion you give your reader is the result of your own thinking.

Too many young people have been told that they are too young to have an opinion. Ridiculous! It is part of the process of growth to form and express opinions. The depth of the opinion will be determined by the experience and reading that your age allows you, but that doesn't take a single degree of importance from your thoughts.

It is also true that an opinion you feel justified in holding today may change tomorrow because of further reading or studying. That doesn't necessarily mean that your original thought should be held in contempt, simply that you have grown in your thinking. You have extended your reading and your studying to the point that you see the fallacy of the first opinion. Fault lies in one's refusal to see an error in thinking that prevents one from accepting demonstrated truth, or in one's eagerness to change opinions quickly in an effort to end up on the right side. The only question you must answer is what caused you to make the change. Was it authoritative information or a whim? Whims don't count, but an educated change is wisdom.

Opinions vary in type:

Interpretation deals with the significance of the subject. By using interpretation, you will explain the meaning of a condition, another's opinion, an action, a book or other piece of writing. Interpretation will not be fact, of course, because another's interpretation of the same material may not agree with yours, but it will be as close to fact as you can come in your viewing of the subject.

Evaluation answers the questions: What is its value? Is it good or bad? Is it worthy or unworthy? We evaluate constantly in our thinking, weighing many of our thoughts automatically: Is this milk rich? Is Davis a good superintendent? Is a stop sign at Third and Main worth the expense? Is the new tax proposal a good idea? What is the value of brotherly love?

To arrive at your judgment, you will want to study the reasons behind the thought or action you are evaluating: What is the average or standard on which you base your judgment? Is there authority to prove that standard? Do you accept it?

You might consider the question: Are the highways well kept? Compared to what? Where? Is the condition of the highway better than that average highway you have made your standard? You might evaluate the statement: Joan is happier today. Happier than whom? John? Her family? Her general attitude toward the world? You must make a comparison. Using this information as a measuring stick, you will reach your judgment or evaluation.

Subject

Subjects for Opinion papers are unlimited. They may range from modern-day manners and changes in fashions to the concerns of business and the national economy. You might discuss violence on TV or the value of psychic readings. An Opinion paper might focus on modern art, diets, environmental pollution, or the pollution of the mind. Or it may be a pet peeve you want to send the Forum in the local newspaper. Everyone has some kind of opinion on all those subjects that flit across the screen of the mind, so choose something that interests you and interpret it or evaluate it.

Preparation and Writing

In Part I, you learned that once you have chosen a subject, you must narrow it down to express the one idea that you want to point out to your reader. To assure yourself of the specificity of your purpose, write out your Statement of Purpose on a notecard and underline the Controlling Idea.

Your next step is to survey your file drawers—Memory, Library, and People—to make sure you have sufficient material on the subject. Even though this paper is written to reflect your opinion, you'll want authorities and facts to back you up. Facts shore up your own ideas and opinions, giving you, an unknown, the support you will certainly need.

Follow the instructions for using notecards. The basic steps are as follows:

- Make a Bibliography card for each source
- Write each idea on a separate card, identifying it as to source number and topic
- Sort the cards into three Main Points with their accompanying minor supports
- Arrange the outline

Once the outline is completed and arranged in a sequence that is entirely logical, write the whole paper without stopping to make a correction, thereby capturing the spontaneity of your thoughts. You'll have plenty of time in the rewriting stage to tighten the flow of words and correct spelling, punctuation, and thinking errors.

This is an Opinion paper, your opinion, but it must be written fairly and with courtesy and good taste. You must gain the confidence that comes from solid research and study so that

your writing takes on a firm, authoritative style. You hope that
by impressing your reader with your opinion, you will stimulate
him to think about the subject and consider or reconsider his
own opinion. This effect is a mighty responsibility for a writer
and should be held in respect. Weigh the facts you select to
determine whether or not you *can, should,* or *must* say certain
things, give certain facts, reach certain conclusions. Understand
your own view on the subject, and with judgment—not prejudice—face the reasons for your viewpoint. Present your ideas
and support them with research and thought. Be accurate and
fair. Don't color or slant your writing for the sake of shock or
emotionalism.

Opening

Interesting material on a general level will open the first
paragraph. If you choose to open with a story, make sure that
it is vivid, interesting, and directly to the point of your Purpose.
Such a story should capture the reader's interest and lead him
on into the article. This first paragraph, then, becomes the
Opening.

Beginning

For the Beginning paragraph, continue with broad, more
general ideas, and gradually narrow the scope of the sentences
as you progress to the last sentence of the paragraph. If you've
decided to dispense with an Opening, make sure the first sentence of your Beginning is a provocative statement that will
attract your reader. The last sentence, in either case, will be
your reworded Statement of Purpose.

Sometimes it is difficult to keep the Statement of Purpose
from appearing to be a last-minute tag-on. If this is the case,
check to make sure that your generalizations are really pertinent to the Controlling Idea. Each sentence moves out of the

preceding one and should narrow in content until you reach the lead-in to the Statement of Purpose. This inverted progression must appear natural, expected. You might try working backwards, listing on scrap paper general subjects that seem to flow out of the Statement of Purpose. Then arrange the pertinent ideas in the most effective sequence and write the first paragraph again.

Ending

Now, write the Ending. The first sentence of the final paragraph is a freshly worded Statement of Purpose, not standing baldly alone but woven into a transitional sentence. It must remind the reader of the purpose and yet signal to him that he has reached the destination you promised. You'll want to leave the subject as interestingly as you went into it, so begin to broaden your ideas, a reverse of the movement of the first paragraph.

You may briefly summarize the Middle of the paper or refer to the Beginning. Or you may end with a quotation that will make a strong impact or an anecdote that will leave the reader thinking or smiling.

Select the conclusion that is dictated by your subject and your purpose. If you feel satisfied with the Ending, the reader will too.

Middle

The Middle section is devoted to proving your viewpoint. Here is your opportunity to develop the strength of your argument or opinion, moving logically from one point to the next.

Think of the outline of an Opinion paper as a collection of blocks and angles. The Opening is in the form of a block, the Beginning, a V (or an angle resting on its apex). The Middle consists of block forms, each block representing a paragraph and governed by the order of movement you feel is most effective. The number of blocks depends on the number of Main Points and supports and the length of the total paper. To lengthen a paper, remember, is not to work out more Main Points and minor supports, but is to go more deeply into the subject by strengthening and elaborating the minor supports. One Main Point may have two or more paragraphs of supporting ideas.

How do you plan to use the supports? Obviously, a Main Point proves or explains the Controlling Idea in your Statement of Purpose. Minor supports, then, must explain or support a Main Point, always in terms of supporting the Controlling Idea. Every sentence, every paragraph must point directly to the Controlling Idea. If one does not, delete it. You haven't enough space to indulge in ideas outside the immediate subject area.

An Opinion must be presented in a tactful manner, allowing the reader the freedom of accepting or rejecting your side of the issue as he sees fit. This does not mean that you must timidly ease your way through the subject. Be direct, firm, authoritative, but let the reader know that you have researched both sides of the question and that you have formed your judgment only after weighing all the information. In this way, you are presenting your reasoned opinion, not a prejudice.

At the outset, therefore, you must let your reader know that you are aware of the other side of the issue. You must be willing to admit a point in favor of the "con." You can do this in one or two sentences if you are writing a short paper. If it is a long paper, you may use one or two paragraphs. Once you've addressed the opposing view, however, do not refer to it again. Your opinion is the "pro" of the subject, and the Purpose of the paper, so you are going to devote your time to supporting your point of view.

Remember to save the strongest argument for last. None of your arguments should be weak, but in the pattern of a series, build from the first support through to the strongest argument you have for the Statement of Purpose you've selected.

When you have completed your first draft, check the paper against the following questions:

- Does the paper develop logically?
- Is it interesting to read?
- Have you smoothly woven the thread of the Controlling Idea, from Beginning statement through Middle paragraphs to Ending statement?
- Is the final paragraph satisfactorily conclusive?
- Have you fulfilled the promise in the Statement of Purpose?
- Would you read the paper if it were printed in a magazine?
- Are the mechanics of your paper correct (logic, spelling, grammar, level of language)?

LIBRARY

The Library paper can be one of the most interesting papers you'll write. It is special, for it indicates the best in selecting, evaluating, and merging findings into a meaningful presentation. You will draw information from all three file drawers and will find such unexpected, exciting material that by the time you have completed your work, you will be a mini-expert in the field.

Research is not confined to the student fulfilling a school assignment or to the professional researcher. It is for politicians, lawyers, speakers, business people, writers, ministers, housewives, serious readers—all who want to write their findings in papers which can be shared.

At first glance, you may feel that you will be contributing little or nothing to the paper, as your job is to research the ideas of others, and compile and arrange them in a readable pattern. In part, this is true. However, it is you who determines the

Statement of Purpose and selects the Main Points. It is your interpretation of the findings you are presenting, your opinion you are supporting, your statement you are proving. Through your comments and word patterns you weave the material into a logical and comprehensible whole. You might not draw new conclusions, but the viewpoint you take is all yours—fresh, thoughtful, and unique. You contribute a great deal to this paper.

The various steps for the Library paper, outlined below, were treated at length in Part I, as they provide a useful basis for many types of papers. In the following discussion, we will treat each step briefly and will then refer you to the pages in Part I where you'll find a detailed discussion.

Subject

Choose a subject that intrigues you. You will be spending so much time researching material that you'll want to be sure you can maintain an interest in the subject for that length of time. Look for a fresh treatment if the subject is a weary one used by many. Compare, contrast, prove, inform, question. Choose something contemporary or from ancient times. Think, and you are bound to come up with a subject that is different from the usual.

If, however, you are assigned a subject by your teacher or superior, you must study the assigned or suggested focus. Define the Statement of Purpose on that basis and generate your own interest. If you approach the work with the determination that you are going to enjoy it, you are certain to find the experience worthwhile. (See pages 10–11.)

Statement of Purpose

No paper can be built without a strong focal point or target. It is this target that helps you focus your research on material that proves your point or fulfills your promise; it is this target that is the very heart of your paper.

Take time in determining exactly what you plan to tell the reader, what it is that you want to get off your chest. Pinpoint the Controlling Idea. (See pages 10–15.)

Research

Many beginning writers use the encyclopedia as their main source of information. Encyclopedias are excellent for background information when you begin your research, but they should be used only as a springboard to more in-depth investigation. The encyclopedia is a compilation of digests, and unless you know a great deal about your subject, you will glean only the bare facts. If you are writing a class assignment, check with your teacher; he may allow you to use but one encyclopedia as a source. In most cases, however, you will want to go to as many different sources as is feasible. The entire research process is covered in detail in Part I. (See pages 15–29.)

Organizing, Outlining and Writing

The Library paper is more complex than any other type of paper. First you must go through the process of researching the subject. Then you must carefully organize all the material and arrange your cards into a logical outline. Finally, using your own words, you must weave all your findings into a smooth paper that expands, explains, and proves the Statement of Purpose. All these steps are given in full detail in Part I. (See pages 39–43.)

Beginning

Carefully select the material that best introduces your subject, and write it in such a way that the reader is compelled to read on. Establish your Statement of Purpose and suggest the importance of the subject. (See page 45–46.)

Ending

The Ending is the conclusion, the moment when you tie up all the loose ends, summarize the Main Points, or promise something new. Take the time to be logical. You want to leave the reader with a feeling of satisfaction at having spent his time reading a well-written paper. (See page 46–47.)

Middle

As in most types of papers, and especially in the Library paper, you will determine the three Main Points that will fulfill the promise in the Statement of Purpose. Remember that you may extend each Main Point into several paragraphs, depending on the depth, and length, of your discussion.

Aim for a balance. Each Main Point should have approximately the same depth and expansion as the others, for each is equally important. Remember to save the strongest point for last. (See pages 47–48.)

Segments.   Writing a complete 2,000- to 3,000-word paper can be a frightening undertaking. You look at all the notes you've taken, even after they are organized and outlined, and you ask yourself what in the world you can do next. You know what your purpose is, but you can't keep a clear picture of the total paper in your mind.

Think in terms of small segments. You'll remember that you wrote the Beginning, then the Ending—two small segments of the paper—and that it was quite easy. Use the same approach for the Middle. Think of each Main Point with its minor supports as a section, and write each one separately. You'll be able to keep the direction of such small segments clearly in mind and feel the progress.

Now, line up the segments and add transitions so that one paragraph moves smoothly and intelligently into another. This method can and should be used, regardless of the length of the paper.

Typing Instructions for Footnotes

If you are using the footnote method (and it is quite likely you are) make a backing sheet to help you gauge the space you must leave at the bottom of the page for footnotes.

The backing sheet may be made on a sheet of fairly heavy typing paper. Number each space on the right-hand side of the paper as close to the edge as you can, beginning at the top with number 66 and numbering in descending order to the bottom. When you arrange your paper and carbon, place this backing sheet with the numbers extended on the right beyond your typing paper.

As you type your manuscript, each time you come to a point of documentation you can refer to the numbers on the backing sheet to help you allow room at the bottom of the page for the corresponding footnote. (Before beginning to type the paper, type each full footnote on a separate page so that you'll know exactly how many lines to allow on the final copy.)

Remember that footnotes are single spaced with a double space between footnotes.

If you have a margin of 1½ inches around the page, then you know that the bottom footnote must end 10 spaces from the bottom of the page. Using your backing sheet as a measure, compute that point. Count the total number of lines needed to accomodate the footnotes for that page, including spaces between footnotes and two additional lines for the double space and 1½-inch line that separates the first footnote from the text.

Sounds complex, doesn't it? It isn't, really. From your rough draft, you can figure the superscripts and approximate how many footnotes you will need on the page.

Let's take a look at such a page:

At the end of all material taken from sources you will use a superscripts to indicate a footnote which will identify the source.[5] You should have at least one footnote on each page of your paper,[6] and if you have researched your subject properly, you will probably have more.[7] There is no excuse for lethargy or for apathy when you reach this point of compiling your documentation.[8]

Continue
       the
           writing
              of
                 your
                    text.
                  .
                  .
                  .
                  . . . . This will

be the last line of your page.

---

[5]This is the first footnote of this page (and the fifth one in this hypothetical paper). It is complete and will use two lines.

[6]Ibid., p. 120.

[7]Again, this is a full footnote or complete footnote and it will usually take up two lines.

[8]This is the last footnote on this page. It may use the full two lines, or if the title or publisher's name is longer than usual, it may use three lines.

NOTE: *Keep carbons of your papers!* No matter how careful a professor may be, or a friend to whom you gave the paper for criticism, your work may still get lost. Make a copy of everything important you write. If you submit your work to an editor, keep a carbon. The editor, too, will be as careful as possible with your work, but editors get dozens of pieces of mail every day, mail that goes through the hands of many people. Seldom do any of these people lose a paper, but that first time can be traumatic for you. It takes but a moment to insert a carbon and second paper, and it is certainly worth it. Suggestion: File your carbon copy where you can easily find it if the need should arise.

Format

The Library paper has a format, a certain arrangement or assembly of the divisons. This format can include all the possible divisions or it may be simplified to include only those divisions required of the length and depth of your paper. You will not be preparing a doctorate from instructions in this book, since the required formats are highly specialized and are covered in books that deal solely with formal papers. Here we will discuss formats from the standpoint of your need: the arrangement of the shorter Library paper. The basic divisions are listed below and samples of preliminary pages are illustrated in the figures that follow.

1. *Preliminaries* (numbered in small Roman numerals: 1 = i; 2 = ii; 3 = iii; and so on).
   a. Cover page (see Figure 7).
   b. Second page—blank sheet of paper.
   c. Title page (see Figure 8).
   d. Table of Contents—to be included if you have chapter divisions or headings you want to find with ease. The length of the Table of Contents will vary according to the divisions of your paper and may require more than one page. In a short paper without significant headings, it may be omitted entirely (see Figure 9).
2. *Text* (numbered in Arabic numerals beginning with 1).
   a. Introduction—if you need to explain unusual circumstances that caused you to choose your subject or if you need to explain your methods of gathering material.
   b. Main body of the paper—usually consists of well-

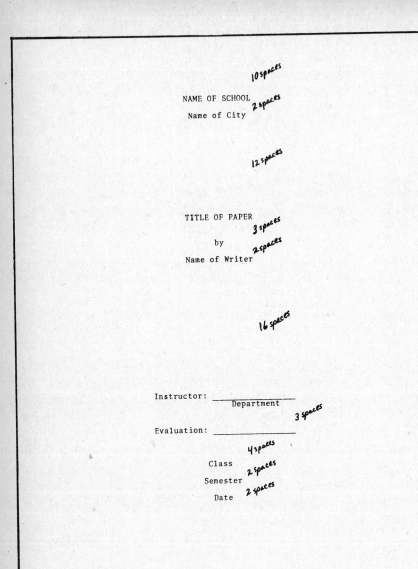

NAME OF SCHOOL   *10 spaces*
Name of City   *2 spaces*

12 spaces

TITLE OF PAPER   *3 spaces*
by   *2 spaces*
Name of Writer

16 spaces

Instructor: _____
Department   *3 spaces*
Evaluation: _____

Class   *4 spaces*
Semester   *2 spaces*
Date   *2 spaces*

Figure 7.   Cover page

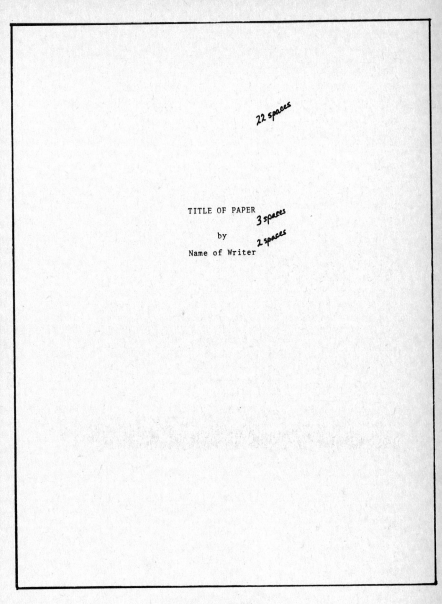

Figure 8. Title page

TABLE OF CONTENTS

Figure 9.   Table of Contents

defined divisions, such as chapters or their equivalents. If you are working with a short paper, you will not be concerned with such divisions but will write the paper as a single unit (see Figure 6 on page 54).

3. *References* (numbered consecutively in Arabic numerals following the last page of the text).

   a. Bibliography of sources (see pages 34–36 for sample formats).

   b. Appendix—If you have scales, tables, maps, and other materials that are important but not a part of the text, place them in this division.

QUERY LETTER

A Query Letter is a simple letter of inquiry. Nothing more. Its simplicity, however, does not lessen its importance. It is the standard method for acquainting an editor with your ideas for an article, a potential employer with your qualifications for a position, or some other individual with your interest in contacting him. If it is a manuscript query, you are asking if you may send the completed piece of writing. If you are writing for some other purpose, you are usually asking to meet the recipient of your letter for an interview concerning that purpose.

Such a request indicates that you want to make the best impression you can, which means you want to send a neat, to-the-point, well-composed letter. As you write, think of yourself as seated across the desk from the recipient, quietly explaining to this very busy person what ideas or capabilities you have that are of unique interest to him.

Manuscript

If you are interested in getting your writing published, a Query Letter is a must. It opens the door for you. "Over the transom" material—unsolicited or not referred to the editor by an agent or other professional—will not receive the VIP treatment. In fact, the material is often returned without a reading.

If the editor is interested in what you tell him in your query, he will invite, or solicit, you to send the completed piece. This invitation does not mean a sale, but it does mean that your article will get a reading.

Be sure to include an SASE (self-addressed stamped envelope) if you want your manuscript returned to you if it is rejected.

The Query Letter follows the same basic pattern of all papers: Beginning, Middle, Ending.

Beginning.   The first paragraph should introduce your article by giving the title and a brief overview of its contents. What is the purpose of the article? What does it do for potential readers? Remember, you aren't trying to tell the editor his business. Don't try to impress him with your great ability to write or tell him that your subject is one he can't afford to pass up. He's probably been in business longer than you have been writing, and although you may not always agree with his decisions (especially if he doesn't buy your article), he's getting paid to make them, not you. Simply, interestingly, convincingly, acquaint the editor with your article. Know that the merit of the article itself will clinch the sale if he invites you to send it.

Middle.   The middle section should give the editor some of the highlights of the piece. It should let him know whether or not you are using anecdotes, case histories, quotations. State clearly the mood of the article: whether or not it is factual, controversial, humorous, and so on. State whether or not you are using excerpts from other printed material. Such excerpts may require clearances and permission fees, so it is wise to keep them to a minimum. You might include a short excerpt from the article, say a paragraph.

Be sure to let the editor know your qualifications for writing on your subject. Are you blowing smoke or do you have a substantive foundation for what you are saying? These qualifications do not have to appear in any one paragraph. If they "feel" better in the first paragraph, weave them in. If your qualifications fit in best with the material you plan for the second or even the third paragraph, place them there, but do include them. Be clear and entirely honest. An editor is not going to think seriously about an article on solar heat if the writer is unknown, or barely skims the surface of the subject, or writes as if he were exposing a pet peeve and nothing more. He wants facts, authoritative proof, or he won't buy. Be sure of where you stand, sure of the truth, and willing to clearly prove your points. Can you? Then tell him you can.

Ending. In the final paragraph, indicate the number of words in the article and ask the editor if you may submit the entire piece so that he can judge for himself if it is right for his publication.

The Beginning Writer. For the beginning writer, one who is not known in the writing field, it is wise to use the preceding query format as a cover letter, omitting the brief excerpt in favor of sending two or three pages from your actual article. The first and last page, or the first, second, and last page should be enough to acquaint him with your style of writing and manner of presenting your material.

Application

If your query has to do with possible employment, the letter serves to introduce yourself, to show your interest in the job, and to present your qualifications.

Of course, along with your letter you will want to send a résumé showing a brief record of your education, training, and experience.

Beginning.   If your query concerns an application for a job, loan, or membership, let the reader know specifically why you are writing him. Name the position you are seeking or the purpose of your letter of application.

Middle.   It is the body of your letter that explains—to your potential employer, to the investment company that is going to lend you money, to the club in which you seek membership— why you qualify. Show your interest. Tell why you think you qualify. Have you any special training? Do you excel in some area that would be of interest or pertinent to the purpose of your communication? Have you won any awards for your work in this field? Do you lecture? Make the recipient of your letter interested in meeting with you. Be factual in what you write but not dramatic.

Ending.   Tell the recipient that you will be glad to meet with him at his convenience for an interview. If you are from out of town and plan to be in the city where his company is situated, tell him so and suggest that you will be available for an interview at that time. Make clear the dates of your visit.

Materials

Use 18- to 20-pound nonerasable bond paper. It has a good texture and takes a sharp type. A logo or letterhead is quite acceptable—if it isn't too flashy or too "smart"—but it isn't necessary. You can send a professional-looking letter by taking care to center your typing on plain 8½ × 11-inch paper.

Leave 1½-inch margins all the way around the page. If you use a letterhead, drop the letter far enough below the printing to keep the page from looking cluttered. Try to fit the letter on one page, certainly not more than two.

Make sure your type is clean. Correct errors with chalk-backed tape or correcting fluid so that the corrections will not be apparent. You must have the letter typed for you if you

cannot type. (Be sure to keep a carbon copy for your records.)
Fold the return envelope—properly addressed and stamped, of
course—and enclose it with your query letter.

Now all you can do is wait, so get busy with your next project.

RÉSUMÉ

A Résumé is an at-a-glance record of your background. The
step-by-step method takes you back to "Getting It Together,"
the subject of Chapter 3 (see pages 39–43), for a Résumé is not
dependent on creative writing so much as on careful organization of information that is cut-and-dried. Its purpose is to introduce yourself and your qualifications to others—a potential employer, a committee considering you for membership or an
official position in their organization, a bank evaluating your
financial status. It acquaints the reader quickly and briefly with
your educational background, training, professional work, personal interests, and personal data. If a particular event in your
life enhances your qualifications, you may mention it on your
Résumé, but any detailing of the event properly belongs in a
cover letter.

Work on the same basis as you did in preparing for any of the
types of papers. That means writing all the information on
individual notecards. Start with your education. List the name
and location of the high school you attended, and the year you
graduated. List the colleges you attended, again giving the
name, location, and years you attended each school. If you graduated from college, indicate the name of the school, the year of
graduation, and the degree you earned. Follow the same format
for any graduate degrees you have earned.

Then list your professional training on cards. Give the name
of the professional schools where you received that training, the
location of the schools, and the years you attended.

Next, make cards for your work experience. Give the name

and location of the employer, the kind of business, the position you held and a brief description of your responsibilities, the years you were employed, and your reason for leaving. (If the reason is personal, you may want to wait until your interview to mention it.)

Now, make cards listing your hobbies, your special interests off the job, and your affiliations. On another card, list your personal data (see Figure 10 for a sample of the information to include).

On a final card, list the references you will send if you receive a request for them. It is quite possible that you will not be asked to furnish references, but offer to provide them. To prepare for that eventuality, select one reference to vouch for your character—a good friend, your minister, or a teacher who knows you well; one to speak for your business stability—your banker or someone respected in business; and two to attest to your professional expertise—your employer, boss, foreman, or department head. Be sure to speak to the people you select as references before you send in their names. Tell them your intentions and ask if they are willing to back you up in this manner. It will take them some time to collect their thoughts and properly write a reference for you. Once a request is made, provide each person with an envelope in which to send their letter—properly addressed to the company and stamped, of course.

If you are applying for a position that will mean leaving the company for which you are currently working, it is wise to indicate in your letter whether or not it is acceptable for your present employer to be contacted concerning your possible move. Such a precaution will save you possible embarrassment.

The following Résumé suggests one sample format for assembling your material. Keep in mind that all outlines are flexible and subject to variation. So adapt the format to meet your requirements and fit the information you are dealing with. Present your material starting with the most recent information and work backward. Make sure you stick to the chronology and

YOUR NAME

Address: Fill in your home address   Phone: (000) 000-0000

PROFESSIONAL EXPERIENCE:

September 1980 to present	Give name of firm where you are employed, name and phone number of your supervisor, and position you hold.
June 1976 to August 1980	Again, give name of firm, name and phone number of your supervisor, and the position you held.

(Usually, a résumé calls for not more than ten years of professional background. If you have had more than two jobs during that length of time, list them as you did those above. After each listing, you may state your reason for leaving the job.)

EDUCATIONAL BACKGROUND:

May 1976	Name college, city, state, and degree earned. (If you have no degrees, or if you have not gone to college, no matter. Omit, and begin with your high school record.)
June 1972	Name of high school, city, state.

PROFESSIONAL TRAINING:

Dates	If you have gone to professional school, give the name of the school, city, state, and certificate earned.

PERSONAL INTERESTS:	Spelunking, numismatics, or whatever hobbies you enjoy. List professional organizations to which you belong, and so on.
PERSONAL DATA:	Date of birth. Marital status.
REFERENCES:	Available on request.

Figure 10. Résumé

do not clutter or confuse the presentation. Let the reader find the information he wants at a glance. Complete sentences give way to the selection of key words and details. Be brief, factual, and specific.

Good luck!

CRITICAL REVIEW

The Critical Review is a variation of the Opinion paper. It expresses your opinion of another's writing. (You would do well to restudy the Opinion paper covered on pages 74–81.) To prepare—yourself and the reader—for your opinion, you must know your material well enough to point out certain features of the writing that will bring interest and give foundation to your opinion.

Need I mention that you must read the book?

Some students try to base their review on a reading of the blurbs and synopsis squibs the publisher has printed on the cover. Some see the movie or ask a friend to "tell the story."

That approach won't work. You must know what you are reviewing. Such a demand need not be a burden—not if you begin reading as soon as you have the assignment. Plan your time. Read the entire book to get the story, then go back through it, taking notes and jotting down ideas. If the author writes certain passages that you think are brilliant, note pages and paragraphs on a piece of paper so that you can go back to the passages when you are ready to write. If you think the story is padded and dull, note some passages you can quote to prove your view. Colorful passages, magical use of ordinary words, an idea that strikes you as unique or supports a thought of your own—these passages are important. Make note of them for later reference.

Go farther: Read everything between the covers of the book.

Glance at the Table of Contents (if you are reviewing a nonfiction book), read the Preface or Introduction, and the thumbnail
sketch of the author.

Do all these things before the last two weeks of the assignment period, and you'll be ready to organize and write.

First, consider the genre, or category, of the book. If you can
choose the book you are to review, don't select a work from a
genre that is foreign to your reading habits. Know your field so
that you can easily discuss the requirements of such a book and
can judge the author's success in meeting them.

If you are assigned a specific book to review, take the time to
research the field sufficiently to enable you to write with some
degree of authority.

You need not concern yourself with such devices as foreshad-
owing and imagery, though they are important. Leave them for
advanced students in literature. You will, however, need to
concern yourself with other ingredients of the book.

Setting and Time

The location of the story and the general year of its unfolding
are important: the South in the 1860s; Italy during World War
II; the planet Yar-tuk in the year 5000; the United States today.

Author

You, the reviewer, should tell the reader something about
the author. "Something" does not mean a quick once-over-
lightly from a *Who's Who* in writing. Nor does it mean you
should richly research and spend considerable time writing
the author's biography. Tell the reader what other books in
the genre the author has written. Is there a commonality
among his books? For example, does the author use the same
setting or period or theme? The reader will also want to know

something of the author's stature in the literary world. Don't bother with his date of birth or with information about his parents unless that information is directly related to the subject of the book.

Is there anything in the author's life that would urge him to write this book? For instance, Hemingway wrote of settings where he had lived, of people and environments he knew, and of his philosophy of life.

Characters

Do you identify with any of the characters? Do you care for them? Do you hate them? How do they speak? If the author has been able to show them to you as real, flesh-and-blood people, you'll feel you know them. They will be believable.

Be prepared to show the reader these "people" by using brief excerpts from the book. Excerpts from the book you are reviewing are documented by placing the page number in parenthesis at the end of the excerpt. All excerpts from sources other than the book you are reviewing should be documented in the usual manner (see Chapter 2). If an excerpt is longer than four lines, be sure to indent the left margin the same number of spaces that you indent the first sentence of each paragraph, and type the excerpt single spaced.

Focus and Plot

A book review is neither a retelling nor a summarizing of the plot or the story. It is written to draw attention to the intent of the author and the merits of his work. Perhaps the characters carry the story, and the author has taken great care to put depth into their personalities. The point of emphasis may be the setting or time or a particular problem. Whatever the focus, it should be illustrated through the use of excerpts with accompanying brief explanations.

The actual plot developed by the author may be covered satisfactorily in two or three sentences.

Style

What is style? "Proper words in proper places make the true definition of a style," wrote Jonathan Swift. An author's style is his choice of words, the manner and pattern in which he arranges them, and the quality of his choices.

What, then, is the style of your author's writing? Is it clipped as in the works of Hemingway? Poetic as in some of the shorter books of Leigh Bracket? Spiritual? Terse and hard-hitting? Is it complex as in a Dickens novel? Is it offbeat? Is the style distinctively the author's? Show the reader something about the way the author uses language and structures the flow of his thoughts.

Purpose

Did the author state his purpose in the book or is it implied? What is his purpose? Is it couched in a Universal Truth—one common to all times and peoples? If so, what is the Universal Truth? Did the author develop the theme so that it is clear and satisfying to you?

Most important, did he accomplish what he set out to accomplish?

Your Opinion

Now, here comes the section you've been waiting for: your opinion. What did you think of the book? Did you enjoy it? In answering, don't brush the question aside by saying, "Yes, I enjoyed the book." The reader wants to know more than that. Did the book fill some need of yours? Did it amuse you? Did it make you think? Did it make a strong impact on you? If you disliked the book, what attitude did the author take that turned you off?

Be very careful not to indulge your own wit and brilliance at the expense of an honest appraisal of the book. The focus is not on you but on the author and the book you are reviewing.

A word about fairness, honesty, and accuracy in reviewing another's work. To shrug off a book because you didn't happen to like it is not a basis for a Critical Review. Disagreeing with the author, disliking his slant or approach to the subject, not enjoying his style—these are honest reactions that you can and should express. The important thing is that you remain fair and unprejudiced in expressing your opinion. Support your opinion with excerpts from the author's writing.

Treat your review much the same as does the teacher who reviews your work. Often the teacher may not agree with your subject, but if you present your thoughts in good taste, in a well-organized pattern, he'll judge your work on the clarity of your ideas and your style of expression. You have a right to your opinion, and that right will be honored if you are sincere in what you say.

Balance

Balance your writing. Don't spend five pages telling why you do or don't like the book and leave two pages to cover the rest of the review. Begin with a thorough review of the book and save your opinion for one of the final paragraphs. The implied opinion that is bound to creep into your discussion will lead to your opinion paragraph.

Length

The Critical Review need not be a long paper. By carefully choosing the important points and selecting the words that will clearly "paint" the picture, you can write a fine review in four typewritten pages, or approximately 1,000 words.

If you have planned your time properly, you'll have time to let the paper rest a few days. When you pick it up again, read the material aloud. You'll be amazed how errors in your writing stand out when you hear the paper read. You'll also enjoy the portions that are very well written.

Divisions

The Critical Review is divided into the Beginning, the Body (or Middle), and the Closing.

Beginning. Give the name of the author and the title of the book you are reviewing. Of course, you've provided this information on the title page, but it must be given again in the text of your paper. Provide some information about the author and point out the relationships of this book to other works the author may have written.

If any of the author's interests show in the writing of the book, explain how they are used.

Body. Begin by telling the reader something of the author's style of writing. Does he use dialogue or interior monologue? Is his language sharp, sweeping, foul, colloquial, scholarly?

How do the characters appear? How do they react? Are they vague or clear-cut? Don't list all the characters in the book, but do show the reader the protagonist, the antagonist, and the most interesting or significant secondary characters. Brief glimpses, mind you, are all you need. How do the characters fit into the book?

Tell the reader what the author's purpose is and whether or not he succeeded in fulfilling that purpose. Did he use a Universal Theme? If so, what is it, and how is it expressed within the story? (Use excerpts to prove your statements. Again, keep them brief and to the point.) Does the author use the same theme in any of his other books?

Explain how the author uses description. Some authors are able to suggest description beautifully through the dialogue and action of the characters. Others include paragraphs of description alone. Did the author sometimes stop the progress of the story to describe? If he did, was it irritating or was there such magic in his words that you were never really aware of the pause in action? Show the reader how the author accomplishes such an effect.

Closing.   The reader is interested in what professional critics have said about the book, about the author, and about his standing in the writing community. Find some professional reviews of the book and use a quotation or two. Be sure to document the quotes. Again, go to Chapter 2.

What is your opinion of the book? Do you think it is a good book? Why? What makes it worthy of a place in literature or on the category shelves? Is there beauty or impact?

If you don't like the book, specify why don't you like it. Do you think that, in spite of your dislike, the book is worthy of being on the library shelves? Why? Does it have any kind of message for someone else? Is it a waste?

Finally, sum up your evaluation in the final sentence. Don't belabor it. Be concise, fair, and honest. When you have done this, stop. Nothing more need be added.

PART THREE
LEST YOU'VE FORGOTTEN

6

SENTENCES

Isolated words aren't much in the way of communication. "Stand," "Go," "Come," and the like, can be used, but you'll have to admit such "sentences" limit communication. Sentences made up solely of verbs are far too Spartan to be interesting.

Not until early people began to put words together to form complete thoughts and sentences did language as we know it come into being. Now, we use sentences almost from the time we learn to speak and it is almost irritating to think in terms of learning how to structure a sentence. Why should we bother? We make ourselves understood, don't we?

In speech, utterance is only one aspect of expressing a thought. Inflection, gestures, stance all contribute to the meaning. As a result, we speak in a kind of verbal shorthand, and we are understood.

It is quite different, however, when we write. Here, the meaning of a thought is expressed entirely by the use of words in a particular sequence and punctuation to clarify phrases and clauses. An understanding of structure, then, is essential if we intend to make the thought entirely clear, to hit the target directly. To work with the words that make up a sentence, we must first understand what a sentence is.

DEFINITION: A sentence is a group of words expressing a complete thought. It consists of two parts: the subject (that part about which something is said) and the predicate (which says something about the subject).

The subject is expressed through the use of a noun, a pronoun or a verbal. The predicate is expressed in a verb, which can show existence("is"), action ("ran"), or occurrence ("think").

To find the subject of a sentence, look first for the verb. Then ask yourself, Who or what acted or was acted upon? The answer to that question is the subject of the sentence.

TYPES OF SENTENCES

There are four *types* of sentences: declarative, imperative, interrogative, and exclamatory. This classification is based on the meaning the sentence expresses or the purpose it fulfills.

A *declarative sentence* makes a statement that may be either true or false:

The use of the word *scale,* meaning "ladder" or "staircase," is obsolete.

An *imperative sentence* expresses a command or makes a request:

Tell me the capacity of the bus.

An *interrogative sentence* asks a question:

Who is your favorite author?

An *exclamatory sentence* expresses strong feeling or emotion:

What a beautiful sunset!

KINDS OF SENTENCES

There are four *kinds* of sentences: simple, compound, complex, and compound-complex.

Simple Sentences

The basic structure of all sentences is the simple sentence. It is the nugget at the core of even the most complicated sentences.

DEFINITION: A simple sentence consists of one independent clause and no subordinate clauses.

It may be a subject-verb sentence:

June sings beautifully.

or it may be a subject-verb-object sentence:

The batter slammed the ball.

It takes no brilliance to realize that sentence after sentence built along this subject-verb or subject-verb-object pattern courts interest disaster. There is no easier way to turn off a reader —peer or professor—than to write with this lack of variety. Elaboration is the key to sentence variety and reader interest. It will help color the thought you are expressing in a simple sentence. There are four basic tools of elaboration: prepositional phrases, verbals, appositives, and compound subjects and verbs.

Prepositional phrases. You know what prepositional phrases are, don't you?

DEFINITION: A preposition (a word showing a relationship) and its object (a noun or pronoun following it) form a unit, a prepositional phrase. This unit is used as an adjective or adverb modifier.

Put your paper <u>on</u> my desk.

Jane and I live the same distance <u>from</u> work.

I enjoy playing the organ <u>in</u> the chapel.

PREPOSITIONS

about	behind	from	toward
above	beneath	in	under
across	beside	into	until
after	between	of	up
against	beyond	off	upon
along	by	on	with
among	down	over	within
around	during	past	without
at	except	through	
before	for	to	

Verbals.   Verbals are not difficult modifiers to use, though they can sometimes be a little tricky. If you study the examples carefully, you're sure to catch on quickly.

DEFINITION: Verbals are verb forms—gerunds, participles, and infinitives—that can be used as nouns, adjectives, or adverbs.

<u>Swimming</u> is great fun. *(Gerund)*

A <u>laughing</u> man is a happy man. *(Participle)*

They stopped <u>to help us.</u> *(Infinitive)*

A *participle* is a verb form that is used as an adjective. As a *present participle* it ends in *-ing,* as in laughing, jumping, lifting. The past participle usually ends in *-ed, -t, -d, -en,* or *-n,* as in filtered, lost, held, stolen, blown.

Participial phrases may also be formed and used as adjectives. They contain a participle and additional modifiers:

Throwing off his coat, Matt prepared himself for the fight.

A *gerund* has the same form as the present participle, thus ending in *-ing*. The gerund, however, is used as a noun:

Singing gives me great satisfaction.

Gerund phrases may also be used:

Proofreading your papers is a habit you should cultivate.

The infinitive is the third verbal form. This verb form is usually preceded by *to*. The infinitive can be used as a noun:

To fly a jet was Ted's only ambition.

as a modifier:

He tried to avoid work.

or with modifiers to become a phrase:

His goal is to write a television script for the show *Vegas*.

Appositives.   Appositives offer another simple way to add variety to your sentences.

DEFINITION: An appositive is a noun—often with its modifiers —set beside another noun or pronoun to explain or identify it.

Your friend Jill won the beauty contest.

"Jill" is a *restrictive appositive*. That is, the appositive is so closely related to the word "friend" that no punctuation is required or necessary. The word "Jill" is essential to the clarity of the sentence.

> Gerald Hay, <u>president of the Pharmaceutical Corporation,</u> is a good friend of my father's.

In this sentence the underlined words form a *nonrestrictive appositive*. It is interesting to have this identification of the man, but it is nonessential information. Moreover, the information is not essential to the grammatical structure of the sentence. A nonrestrictive appositive is set off by commas.

Compound subjects and verbs.   Compounds are perhaps the most commonly used forms of elaboration.

DEFINITION: A compound subject is one in which two or more subjects—connected with *and* or *or*—have the same verb. A compound verb is one in which two or more verbs—connected by a conjunction—have the same subject.

> The <u>jockey</u> (s-1) and the <u>trainer</u> (s-2) discussed the possibility of winning the race.

> He <u>has gone</u> (v-1) without sleep for two nights and <u>looks</u> (v-2) as if he were about to collapse.

Compound Sentences

Compound sentences make up a very small percentage of our written material.

DEFINITION: A compound sentence consists of two or more main clauses that are capable of standing independently but are joined together in equal grammatical rank and pattern.

She rang the doorbell, but no one came.

She rang the doorbell; no one came.

She rang the doorbell; however, no one came.

Notice the different effects of the three compound sentences in the preceding example. Two main clauses are used in each sentence. The only variation is in the use of connective devices.

In the first sentence, the coordinating conjunction *but* joins the two main clauses.

COORDINATING CONJUNCTIONS

and	nor
but	or
for	so
	yet

In the second sentence, no connecting word is used. The semicolon takes the place of the comma and coordinating conjunction.

The third sentence shows another variation of the compound sentence. In this sentence, a semicolon and the conjunctive adverb *however* are used. The conjunctive adverb acts as a connective and is generally followed by a comma.

CONJUNCTIVE ADVERBS

accordingly	hence	nevertheless
also	however	nonetheless
besides	indeed	then
consequently	likewise	thus
furthermore	moreover	therefore

Complex Sentences

Nearly half the sentences in current writing are complex.

DEFINITION: A complex sentence is a sentence made up of one
   independent clause and one or more subordinate clauses.

An *independent* or *main clause* has a subject-verb pattern
and is complete in thought. It could stand alone.

> <u>James had forgotten</u> that <u>it was his idea.</u>

A *subordinate* or *dependent clause* also has a subject-verb
pattern, but is used as a noun or modifier in the same way as are
single words and phrases. Subordinate clauses are joined to an
independent clause by a subordinating conjunction such as *as,
because, since,* or *when,* or by a relative pronoun, such as *that,
who,* or *which.* The subordinate clause cannot stand alone. It
must join an independent clause to complete the thought.

Compound-Complex Sentences

Here's where you get to combine the different kinds of sentences we've discussed.

DEFINITION: A compound-complex sentence is a sentence
   that contains two or more main clauses and one or more
   subordinate clauses.

> Amy walked to school because she liked to talk with her friends
> on the way, but her sister Mary rode her bike because she liked
> the exercise.

SENTENCE VARIATION

- Vary the length of your sentences. Avoid a choppy style
  resulting from a series of short sentences. Often you can
  combine choppy sentences into longer sentences.

- Also avoid long rambling sentences that go on and on until the reader has forgotten the point you were trying to make.
- Vary the beginning of your sentences by using phrases and clauses.
- Use appositives to add variation to the pattern of your sentences.
- Use modifiers to qualify, restrict, and color your sentences. They may appear in any position in a sentence. However, in most cases modifiers should be placed as close as possible to the word they modify.

  Be careful not to tack on a modifier simply for the sake of clever variation. If the poor thing has nothing to modify, it dangles mid-air. Such a modifier is of no use and is always ridiculous:

  Stepping daintily across the floor, the book fell from the table.

- Use correlative conjunctions (coordinating conjunctions used in pairs) for additional variation—both . . . and; either . . . or; neither . . . nor; not only . . . but (also); whether . . . or; though . . . yet:

  They didn't know <u>whether</u> he was at the airport <u>or</u> at the bus station.

The important thing for you to remember is that the reader must never lose interest in what you are writing. That interest starts with you. If you are interested in what you are writing about and really try to get the idea across to your potential reader in a sparkling manner, you'll earn his attention. Remember, too, that your teacher is a reader in this sense. If you make the kind of effort that shows your involvement in the subject, he'll read your paper with interest. A little extra effort in the presentation of the subject will gain his attention, in spite of the many papers he has to read.

SENTENCE FRAGMENTS

If your aim is to leave your reader somewhere up river, cloud your writing with sentence fragments. We're dealing in complete sentences, remember, good old subject-verb patterns. True, many professional writers use fragmented sentences, but if you look closely, you'll find they are used for a specific reason that the writer knows and understands. He knows the rules and breaks them to shock, emphasize, amuse, and so on. You haven't reached the freedom that knowing-the-rules allows. Be patient. You'll get there.

> *Complete sentence:* After the flash flood, the highway was scarred with holes and troughs gouged out by the water.
>
> *Fragment:* After the flash flood.
>
> *Fragment:* After the flash flood, the highway scarred with holes and troughs.

As you can see, a sentence fragment is a group of words that does not express a complete thought. It cannot stand alone, as it doesn't follow the subject-verb pattern, the minimum requirement for a sentence.

I can hear you say, "Oh, now, I never write fragments. I know what a sentence is."

Proofread your work. You may be surprised to discover how often a sentence fragment slips through. Test each sentence to make sure it meets the subject-verb requirement. Don't let a subordinate clause pose as a complete sentence.

> *Fragment:* I was grateful for my financial success. Which enabled me to invest in the new corporation.
>
> *Complete:* I was grateful for my financial success, which enabled me to invest in the new corporation.

RUN-ON SENTENCES

A common fault in writing is the run-on sentence. When you use a comma or a semicolon or a conjunction instead of a period between two complete sentences, you're in trouble. You've created a run-on, a situation in which one complete sentence runs into the next and often the next and the next. This isn't due to a lack of understanding on your part, for you do know better. You've simply allowed yourself to become careless. Know the kind of sentence you want to write and stay within the limits of that structure.

If you're aiming for clarity in your writing, you need to clean up these bits of carelessness. It doesn't take much time, and it really adds merit to your work. Remember, when you come to the end of a sentence—whether it is simple or complex, compound or compound-complex—use a period, exclamation mark, or question mark. Let the reader know that you have completed one sentence and are moving on to the next.

7

PARAGRAPHS

For the purpose of learning how to write a paragraph, think of each paragraph as a mini paper. You must learn to structure your paragraphs carefully to express your ideas and interest the reader. And as in writing a whole paper, you must keep the Statement of Purpose, the central idea of the paper, in mind at all times.

Physically, a paragraph is indented five to seven spaces from the left margin of the page. It signals to the reader that a new idea is coming up, that another support is being presented. When a paragraph tries to cover too many ideas or scoots into little side issues not directly related to the main idea, the reader becomes confused. When one idea stands out and is smoothly supported by related sentences, the reader understands what you are saying and finds the reading pleasant. The construction of the paragraph is the key to writing a clear unit of thought.

It has been said that if you can write a paragraph, you can write a book. While no generalization can stand up in all cases, to a great extent this one is true. The same basic pattern exists in both. The structure of paragraphs is as follows:

Beginning:	Topic Sentence
Middle:	Body
Ending:	Clincher (or transition)

TOPIC SENTENCE

The first step in writing a paragraph is to determine the single idea, the main thought, you want to present to your reader. This may sound like a foolish step, but if you consider all the ideas that tumble through your mind, you will find that most of them take in so much territory that it would be impossible to shoehorn them into a single paragraph.

For instance, you may select Respiratory Diseases as your subject. Now, that covers everything from asthma to emphysema to colds. There is no way you can cover all that in one average paragraph, or approximately 150 words.

So you zero in on colds. Fine. What aspect do you plan to discuss? The pressure and discomfort of head congestion? How about the medical description of a cold? Maybe you want to give step-by-step directions for treating a cold. Remember, you must limit your subject to one specific idea. That is all you can include in a single paragraph.

Once you have decided on the specific idea, the next step is to express it in a single statement, your Topic Sentence. This statement is your promise to the reader of what you will cover in the paragraph. Keep in mind that the idea must be at once rich enough to allow for 150 words of pertinent material and streamlined enough to be covered in one paragraph.

Let's say your interest is in solar energy. What are some of the single aspects you might discuss?

A program for the use of solar energy for heating involves great expense.

A program for the use of solar energy for heating involves much scientific study.

A program for the use of solar energy for heating involves selling the public on its efficiency.

As you can see, there are many single aspects of this vast subject area that can be successfully limited to an interesting paragraph.

Controlling Idea

Once you are satisfied with your Topic Sentence, determine the key words of the statement. This is a very important step. Take time to understand the specifics of what you intend to say.

Look at the preceding sample sentences and study the underlined words. These are the key words. They indicate the Controlling Idea in each sentence. In the first, you will limit your discussion to the cost in maintaining the program. In the second, you will discuss the need for scientific study. In the third, you will talk of having to sell the public on solar heat.

The statement is your Topic Sentence. It contains the Controlling Idea that definitely announces that one thing about which you will write.

Although in advanced writing, the Topic Sentence can appear in the first sentence of the paragraph, in the last sentence, in any logical place in the body, or simply implied, for the purposes of your present work you will place the Topic Sentence at the beginning of your paragraph.

Having determined the Topic Sentence and focused on the Controlling Idea, you are ready to go on to the body of the paragraph.

BODY

Now you must gather all the materials you'll need to support the subject of your paragraph. If you are discussing the expense of the solar energy program, you are not interested in information about scientific studies or techniques for selling the public

on the idea. Your interest lies only with your promise to the
reader: the cost of the solar energy program. That will guide
you in your selection of materials.

List all the points you can think of that will support or prove
your Controlling Idea. Remember that you will be much happier selecting the points you want to include from a long list of
possibilities than puzzling over how you can stretch one or two
points to make the 150 words.

Development

Once you have collected your material, the next step is to
assess your material.

Details. You may opt to use details or facts to develop your
paragraph. If so, break down the Controlling Idea into its com-
ponent parts. For example, suppose you want to tell someone
how to install a dead-bolt lock in a door. As you would in a
How-to paper, you must tell the reader each required step.
Placed in sequence, these steps explain "how" to install the
lock. In the development of the paragraph, you'll take the
reader step by step from the beginning through to the conclusion.

You may decide to relate an experience, such as your first
time ringside at a boxing match. Your accounting of the experience may come through details of sights, sounds, smells, and
emotions.

You may want to discuss an idea that requires documented
facts to prove. Check to make sure the facts you select are
directly related to the Controlling Idea, and be sure to credit
the source from which you took the information.

Illustrations. Illustrations, narrative examples in which
something happens, may also be used for the development of
a paragraph. Show that "happening" to prove your point or
support your idea. Let the reader see the drama unfolding. Give

examples. You may want to use names—not necessarily true names—to make the drama of the illustration more believable.

Reasons. You may decide to use reasons to develop your paragraph. If you do, make sure that you have carefully thought them through. Your professional opinion may give you authority for your reasoning. However, if you are not a professional in the field, check your reasoning with research. Or perhaps your own experience has provided you the basis for your reasoning. Whatever, your reasons must be sound and directly to the point.

How do these three possible developments vary?

Detail is a fact, a part of a whole, a step in a procedure. It tells the *how* and *what* of the idea you are discussing. A detail comes from outside your own mind, from things that have happened in the world about you.

Illustration is a narrative example that explains your Controlling Idea by showing something that has happened. You may develop your idea in one long illustration or you may use several. Make sure, however, that you do not stray from the main purpose of the paragraph. *Reason* is an opinion. You gather all the information, assess it, and determine in your own mind what your opinion is. You answer the question *why* when you use reason.

Minor Supports

You now have the material—details, illustrations, or reasons —that will support your Controlling Idea. These, then, become the major supports of the Topic Sentence.

Let's say you have three solid supports. If you confine the body of your paragraph to these three supports, you'll find you have a dull piece of writing. Though you may have covered the essential points of your subject, you will not have provided enough interest to stimulate the reader to read on. And so you expand. Delve into some of the more specific aspects of the major supports and incorporate this additional material into your paragraph to give more depth to your idea. These added portions are minor supports.

Minor supports apply to each major support and simply define or explain or detail the major idea and add more understanding to the Controlling Idea.

Order of Movement

Up to this point, you haven't placed your information in any particular order; you have simply determined the major supports and taken the time to expand them. You aren't sure of the pattern you'll use. Let's review the possible orders.

Time Order. In a paragraph that entails specific steps—such as explaining a procedure, giving directions, or recounting an experience—a chronological time order should be followed. Start at the beginning of the procedure—baking a cake, shoeing a horse, lifting in a balloon—and follow the procedure through, step by step, to its conclusion.

Space Order. In a paragraph concerning movement covering space—for example, a trip from Los Angeles to New York by way of Canada—you'll want to follow a space order. You can't discuss all the cities along the way, so you'll choose the large or most famous cities to plot your itinerary. You may begin with Los Angeles, move to Denver, on to Winnipeg, and so on.

Or you may be describing the disaster appearance of a friend's living room. Again, you'll plot your itinerary. You might begin by describing the layout of the room left to right and then develop the scene by moving from the mantel to the tabletops to the chairs and finally to the floor. Don't let your description become a disaster by hopping from floor to table to floor to mantel to chair and so on. Decide on the itinerary or pattern and stay with it.

General-to-Specific (Deductive) Order. In expository writing, the general-to-specific order of movement is probably the easiest and most favored order to use. It begins with a broad, general statement, preferably a Topic Sentence so interesting that the reader is forced to read the paragraph. Neither time nor space is of particular importance in this paragraph. The arrangement of the supporting material is strictly your choice. Keep in mind, however, that you are working for an effect: interest, proof, impact, emphasis. You must write to catch and hold the attention of your reader.

For our purposes, we'll use the Topic Sentence at the beginning of the paragraph. It should be a general statement, but sufficiently provocative that the reader will look forward to the material to come.

Then come the supporting sentences which are made up of details, illustrations, or reasons. The order you choose will be the one that makes the most sense of your material.

Remember, a general-to-specific or deductive paragraph moves from the general (Topic Sentence) to the specific (supporting sentences).

Specific-to-General (Inductive) Order. In the inductive order of movement, the paragraph begins with specifics and builds to the general. The Topic Sentence, then, becomes the final sentence. This does not relieve you from writing a first sentence that catches the attention of the reader. You may begin with details, reasons, or illustrations. Just be sure that your specifics point to the final sentence.

Climactic Order. The climactic order of paragraphing is similar to the specific-to-general order, with one exception. Each new idea or new support builds in importance to the final Topic Sentence. Like the climax of a story, the climax of the paragraph creates the impact you want to achieve.

Experiment with these orders of movement. Let your materials tell you which order will present your paragraph with the greatest intellectual or emotional appeal. If you are going to put in the hours it takes to write, have the pride to make those hours pay off.

CLINCHER

Now for the ending. There is no one tried-and-true way to end a paragraph. The way that satisfies the reader is with its completion or fulfillment is the proper way.

If you have written a particularly long paragraph, you may feel that the reader would appreciate a summary, a restating in different words, of the Topic Sentence. This, of course, can be done only when following the deductive order. Such a restatement is called a clincher because it clinches the point supported in the paragraph.

Caution: Don't just tack on a clincher so that you can call it quits. Use the clincher when such a restatement is of value, when it really stamps authority on what you have said. If you can make that restatement in less words than the original Topic Sentence and make it effective, you'll have a much stronger paragraph.

If your paragraph is part of a paper, you might incorporate a transition possibility, a promise of more to come. There is more about that in the early pages of this book.

Just remember, the most satisfying conclusion to your paragraph is the natural completion of your supports. Once you have developed your Controlling Idea and made your point. why go on? Leave it clear and clean.

INDEX